Warrior's Paradigm

Also by Chanel Spencer

I Am The Voice

Love, Mama Volume 1

Love, Mama Volume 2

Brand New Me

Get Up Girl and Win

Life of an Entrepreneur

Success Secrets

Life of Harper

The Adventures of CJ

The Evolution Effect

Our Truth is Not a Lie

Warrior's Paradigm
turning your brokenness into beauty

Chanel Spencer

PUBLISHING
New York

Certain names and identifying characteristics might have been changed, whether or not so noted in the text, and certain character and events have been compressed or reordered.

Warrior's Paradigm 2020 by Chanel Spencer
All rights reserved.
Printed in the United States of America.
For information, address M. E. Publishing,
New York

Maximum Evolution
www.maxevol.com

Designed by Chanel Spencer

The Library of Congress Cataloging in Publication Data
is available upon request.

ISBN 978-1-7349735-2-5

Our books may be purchased in bulk for promotional, educational, or business use.
Please contact M. E. Publishing @
www.maxevol.com
or email Chanel.Spencer@maxevol.com

Dedicated to my grandmother, Bernice Henry, who taught me to be brave, kind, and gentle, but most of all, powerful.

Par·a·digm
: is a standard, perspective, or set of ideas.

Par·a·digm shift
: an important change that happens when the usual way of thinking about or doing something is replaced by a new and different way.

About the Author

Chanel Spencer was born and raised in New York City. Chanel helps women to transform their lives and bring their vision to fruition. She is a firm believer in building one's table and no longer fighting for a seat at someone else's. Chanel is an innovative Speaker, Author, and CEO of Maximum Evolution, specializing in branding and business development. Chanel is also 6x best-selling author, creator of ME Publishing, and the host of the Evolv podcast. Chanel has two small children that motivate her to make the world a better place which has fueled her passion to give back to her community; donating her time, services, and products to survivors of domestic abuse and high risk youth. Her goal is to impact and transform the lives of millions of women to understand the value they all possess and lead the life of their dreams. After successfully achieving her professional goals in the hospitality industry, Chanel walked away from her career to focus on Maximum Evolution full-time.

Chanel is a tenacious force who worked her way up from an accounting clerk all the way to general manager of a major hotel in NYC. Along the way, she has overcome every kind of obstacle you can imagine; she uses her wisdom to help businesses and professionals bypass potential threats by identifying and strengthening their weak areas while expanding on their strengths.

After successfully achieving her professional goals in the hospitality industry, Chanel walked away from her career to focus on Maximum Evolution full-time. Since then, she has developed multiple products, written eight best-selling books (including two children's books), worked with numerous authors, created a publishing company, and works as an executive coach.

Recently titled Ms. New York City, NY for the Ms./Mrs. Corporate America competition in 2021.

Connect with her at www.readytotransformnow.com

 @CHANELSPENCERNOW

Contents

Prelude 10
Warrior's Paradigm 17
The Vessel 21
Beautifully Shattered 28
Love Thy Self 47
Purgatory 64
Patterns 75
Family Ties 92
Lost Love 105
Motherly Love 122
The Blame Game 137
Chameleons 153
M.E. on Zero 157
Deception 168
Nemesis 179
Turning your Brokenness into your Beauty ... 188
Acknowledgements 199

Prelude

The Vessel, an elaborate honeycomb shaped spiral staircase, is the centerpiece of New York City's iconic Hudson Yards. The Vessel changed the city's skyline, adding a complex structure comprised of 16 stories and 154 interconnecting flights of stairs- which demands to be climbed. The interactive art piece was born from the imagination of Thomas Heatherwick and features the Heatherwick Studio as a focal point. People can enjoy new perspectives of the city from 80 landings nestled in the Vessel, allowing participants to experience NYC from different heights, angles, and vantage points. It is a visual paradigm.

A lot of us waste years because we get locked into our vision. We see things from one specific direction and get stuck, unable to look beyond what is staring at us. If we could just step back and see the bigger picture, we can understand how to move past whatever obstacles that seem to be holding us back. Sometimes we need a staircase (or another person) to help us see things from a new perspective. Growth only occurs when we are brave enough to look at our lives honestly, from different focal points. When we are open to experiencing life from different heights, angles, and vantage points, we free ourselves up to align with the person we desire to be.

Everyone wants to change the world, I guess I do too, but not in the way most people would think. I understand the only way we can change the world is to first heal ourselves. If you don't take the time to heal from your past, anything you try to do to change the world will leave you disappointed and exhausted. Once you heal yourself, you can help others heal- sparking real change. Change that will have a lasting impact on the world.

I have beautiful children who are my world and my main motivation. I want my children to see their mom going for her dream so they know, feel, and see that it is possible. I am building a legacy for them. I know they are watching everything and anything I do. I want my son to be a strong, happy, and successful king. I want to provide a smooth path for him. I want my daughter to be a beautiful, strong, and successful queen. I never want my children to doubt their worth.

With my children being the driving force, I launched Maximum Evolution. Every decision I have made since the launch has been fueled by my hopes and plans for their future. They give me the strength and courage to push past my fears, self-doubt, and all the anxiety that comes with building a multi-platform empire. Maximum Evolution is a business development company which has expanded to include ME Publishing, Maximum Beauty, and Evolv- I have worked diligently to build a team that can empower people to align with the vision for their future. I created an avenue for people to successfully take an idea and see it all the way through development, creation, marketing, and sales. I have helped people develop products, personal brands, write books, and be a successful leader. I have helped corporations identify and build on strengths, strategize for future plans, and map out the course to bypass obstacles and threats. I have also developed a training program that will improve team performance and create a place in which each member feels valued, which allows for greater productivity and success.

I began Maximum Evolution for the sole purpose of providing a space for me to walk in my purpose so that I could build a legacy for my family; my children and my children's children. However, since the launch, it has become so much more. Maximum Evolution isn't about me or just one person; it's not even about my family.

Maximum Evolution is about all of us working together collectively to achieve personal greatness; creating opportunities for people to align to their best selves and build from there. Is it scary? YES! Uncomfortable? Even more so! Regardless of the fear factor involved, the reward is so much greater than the regret you will feel if you never take that first step. I would have loved to be able to just blink my eyes and have Maximum Evolution be a multimillion-dollar company, but that's not practical; it takes a lot of hard work, dedication, sacrifice, development, and radical action. For you to be successful at anything, you will need to silence the fear, take the leap, educate yourself on every necessary step you need to build for long-term success, leave comfortability behind, do it afraid, and let go of the illusion of perfection. **"Version one is better than version none"** Lisa Nichols said.

    I have been carrying this book within me for years. I feel like I have been pregnant for years and years; I had to get it out. It was important to share my experiences in hopes to inspire those who have gone through similar journeys. I want you to know you're not alone. I have a story; you have a story. We have all been judged and misunderstood because people don't see the parts of our stories we keep hidden; the battles we have lost and the ones we have won. I am a true believer that all I have gone through is for a purpose. It has to be. If I can help a million people or even just one, I will have full satisfaction. I know there are millions of people who have overcome and even more that are still going through hell. If seeing me or reading my story gives them more faith and strength to know there is a light at the end of the tunnel, then the labor of getting my story on the page has been worth it.

My hope for you, as you read this book, is that you will recognize parts of yourself in my story. I hope to inspire you to heal and know that you are not alone. I want you to know healing looks different for every person, but it's possible for all of us. If you are in a dark and scary place, it is possible to pull yourself out. If you need help, I am here. You are not alone.

1
Warrior's Paradigm

"Every great warrior must learn to endure and overcome the adversities of life."
-Lailah Gifty Akita

I have been at war my entire life. I have gone head to head with every demon imaginable. I have limped off the battlefield of relationships wounded. I have been in combat within myself mentally and emotionally, in the corporate world, fighting for my seat at the table. Every fight has been hard, sometimes feeling almost impossible, but none of the battles I have faced has anything on the battle I have overcome with the way I think about myself and the way I see the world.

A paradigm can be defined as a pattern or way of doing something; it's also a mental representation of how an entity, or person, is structured. I like to think of a paradigm as how we see the world, how we see ourselves, how we perceive others, and their view of us. Until I went on my journey of transformation, my paradigm reflected that of a victim; someone who life is happening to. It took me coming to terms with my past, embracing myself, and believing in the warrior inside of me before I would shift my paradigm from a victim to a victorious warrior- capable of anything and everything.

We will always be at war with something or someone. Are you ready for battle? Do you believe in yourself enough to face your fears and fight for the life you want to live? The only way you can win any war is to embrace the warrior within you, rise up, and stand with confidence, embracing your beauty and strength. Your armor is your vessel, and it will not protect you unless you accept it fully.

Through giving yourself time to heal, you will learn to accept and love your armor. Armed and ready for battle, you will begin to notice the shift in your paradigm- the way you see the world. Slowly, you will begin to view life through the lens of a warrior not a victim. You will be proactive not reactive; strategic not impulsive; confident not fearful. Through training your mind, you will begin to notice you are ready for anything and won't feel the need to make yourself smaller to fit into a world you were made to stand out in.

Repeat after me.

I am strong. I am beautiful. My vessel is ready for battle. I am a warrior.

Welcome to my Warrior's Paradigm

2

The Vessel

Go with the pain, let it take you. Open your palms and your body to the pain. It comes in waves like the tide and you must be open as a vessel lying on the beach, letting it fill you up and then, retreating, leaving you empty and clear.
　　　　　-Anne Morrow Lindbergh

We are all vessels carrying, within us, hopes, dreams, goals, achievements, heartbreaks, disappointments, sadness, and traumas. From the moment of your birth, you are a miniature vessel; made of DNA, chromosomes, genes, traits, a sprinkle of beauty, intelligence, personality, and your destined purpose all collide to create the unique vessel that is you. Here you are- a miniature vessel placed on Earth without a guide or a manual to follow. As you develop, the capacity of your vessel grows with the ability to hold, within it, all that life has to offer. Your life experience creates impressions that will shape your vessel mentally, physically, emotionally, and spiritually. These impressions will dictate how you show up in the world and will be reflected in your choices, lifestyle, views, and thoughts.

I am a firm believer in everything happens for a reason. Every situation we find ourselves in will either expose an area you need to work on or help prepare you for your next chapter in life. Although our life experiences create impressions that dictate our lives, we are also created with the ability to change, grow, and evolve. Regardless of our past, we can choose something different. If we put in the work and learn the lessons life presents us through situations, events, and relationships, we can grow our capacity to see the world in a different way and evolve into the person we choose to be.

I am a vessel. You are a vessel. Each vessel leaves a mark on this world. Every vessel has the ability to impact others. When you embrace yourself and allow others to see your authentic self, you will spark change. This vessel has faced many adversities. I have struggled; I have fought; I have failed; I have won. Every obstacle, every struggle has taught me a lesson which shaped my vessel and created my story.

I am a vessel of hope, representing transformation.

I have endured years of turmoil and fueled by negative thoughts running wild in mind. I was held prisoner by my inner critic while my true self was withering away in a cage I constructed through the years. The cage was supposed to be my safe place; a place to hide from the hurt and pain. It quickly became something else; my refuge turned into a prison. I am a fighter, no, a warrior. I am intelligent and highly motivated. I had to come to terms with the fact that I could be more than one thing at a time. I was both broken and beautiful; a warrior and a prisoner; highly motivated yet paralyzed by fear. One truth didn't make the other one a lie. I was both.

I spent years being overlooked. I waited, impatiently, for someone to make space for me at the table of opportunities. Any space; a chair, a stool, a cushion, it didn't matter. I felt shame for wanting the seat. My place at the table was held over my head, dangling in front of me as if I was a rabbit craving a carrot. I was settling for scraps from a table when I knew I deserved more than just a chair. I am a queen, and a queen is worthy of a throne. I was tired, no, exhausted of trying to prove myself in a world that overlooked women, especially women of color. I excused myself from every place that I was tolerated and decided to create a place in which women were celebrated.

I stepped away and built my own table, creating my own seat. The days of accepting less than I deserve are over. I lead with an empathetic mind and heart. I know my mind and its capabilities. I owed it to myself to create a vision for my vessel and then see it into fruition.

This was selfish at first. I thought I was creating a world in which I could flourish. Then I realized this wasn't just about me. I was creating a space for people who have been overlooked, under-served, and forgotten. I am building an endless table with enough seats for everyone.

Every challenge I had to learn to navigate through revealed a small piece of the puzzle that is my purpose. Every piece helped me realize my power. Looking back, I can see clearly, even in the darkest times of my life, that I was being pulled forward into my destiny. An undeniable strength was being forged deep within my vessel. Every time I thought I had nothing left to give, I was able to tap into a newfound courage. Everything I needed was within, I just had to remember. I had to remember who I am, who I choose to be, and the power I have; when I remember that, I will rise up and face anything.

I have come to appreciate all the things I have been through because it has made me into the woman I am today. I have learned how to align with gratitude and be thankful for each person who has let me down because each occurrence held within it a valuable lesson. Overtime, I have been able to identify the lessons given to me and apply them to my life, which has allowed me to be grateful for the heartache. Your pain is not in vain; in it, you will find its purpose that will help you unlock parts of yourself that will lead you to your destiny.

The journey to your destiny begins with inner healing and self-transformation. Every person has to go through certain experiences and repair work to be ready for the journey. Each experience we go through reveals areas that need attention as well as builds, within us, strength and confidence for the next steps in our journey. Everyone will need to do some work along the way- repairs, maintenance, cleaning, organizing, disposal, removals, and sealing holes. The only way we can take ourselves to the next leg of our journey is if we work on ourselves emotionally, mentally, physically, financially, and spiritually. We must explore all of these areas so we can renew our mind, transform our mindsets, break cycles, deal with bad habits, identify our opportunities, release and forgive everyone – even yourself, and finally, focus on your future self and the person you want to become. No one else can do the work for you or force you to do it; it's all up to you. Only you can turn your brokenness into your beauty.

3
Beautifully Shattered

"The best and most beautiful things in the world
cannot be seen or even touched- they must be felt- felt with the heart."

－Helen Keller

I am flawed.

There, I said it. I, Chanel Spencer, am a flawed human being who cannot measure up to today's beauty standards regardless of the never-ending beauty rituals of manicures, facials, and hair appointments. I am proud to say that I have finally been able to love the reflection staring back at me. Yes, the woman I am now is flawed, but I have accepted each and every flaw as a mark of true beauty. I had to redefine what beauty meant to me.

At one point, looking in the mirror caused me emotional and mental pain. I avoided mirrors and anything that would create a reflection. When I would look in the mirror, I was bombarded with the lies from my inner critic.

My inner critic was skilled at pointing out every place I failed to measure up to the world's standard of beauty. Every time my inner critic spoke, my mind run wild with thoughts in agreement to the criticism filling my head.

My inner critic shouted, "Chanel, your lips are too big. Why is your face so bumpy?" My thoughts agreed; I hate these lips. Why is my skin so bumpy?

Ugh, I hate the stretch marks around my belly button. I need to work out. "Why are your arms so weak?"

Yep, I need to go to the gym. Ugh, I want my booty bigger, maybe I need to start doing squats. "Why are you so skinny?" I need to put on weight.

"Why are your teeth so big?" I should look into braces.

"Why don't you take better care of yourself?" I need to get my legs waxed, hair done, eyebrows threaded, YESTERDAY!

The sound of my inner critic drowned out every other voice, was nagging at me, and was quick to point out any and every imperfection.

Our inner dialogue is like an old record playing in the background; an endless song. When our inner dialogue is set to a negative frequency, the song we hear reminds us of everything we hate about ourselves. Overtime, the soundtrack playing on repeat becomes familiar, comforting even. We are our own worst critics. When your inner dialogue is stuck on a negative frequency, even on days you feel beautiful, one small thing can knock you off your game and cause you to become self-conscious of everything- your outfit, how you feel, and what you look like. Every thought quickly becomes negative.

We allow others to define beauty. We look at the media and try to live up to the edited image of women that appear on TV, the big screen, and in print. We see how the beauty industry defines beauty and quickly decide that we can't and try to measure up. They say beauty is in the eye of the beholder. While yes, this is true, I believe that it is essential for you to know, with every ounce of your being, that you are beautiful. I am beautiful. You are beautiful. We are beautiful. Beauty might be in the eye of the beholder, but we can begin to make a shift in how the world measures beauty if we decide to look at each other, I mean really see each other, and decide the list I started this chapter out with; my big lips, crooked teeth, stretch marks are the very things that make me unique. They are what make me, me, and most importantly, they are what makes me beautiful.

The comparison game is the killer of joy and peace, yet every day, we just can't help ourselves and continually fall into the trap of comparing ourselves to everyone around us. Not only do we compare ourselves to the people featured on the cover of the magazines we stare at while we buy our groceries or online, but we also compare ourselves to our "friends" on Facebook and every other social media outlet that sucks us in. I will be sitting at home in sweatpants and in desperate need of some significant beauty transformation; my eyebrows, hair, and nails all need to be done right now, not to mention, I can't remember the last time I waxed my legs, and I look a mess. While I am procrastinating, trying to do anything to avoid writing, I sit and I scroll. You know you do it too, stop judging me. At any time, I can scroll through Instagram and see perfection being posted all throughout my feed. My insecure scroll could, and usually does, lead me down a rabbit hole of comparison which, if left unchecked, can and usually will lead me into something even more dangerous... self-pity, sprinkled with a little self-hatred. After my mindless scrolling and self-comparison, I typically spend the next hour going through the endless list in my mind of all the ways I can't seem to get my stuff together. I find myself staring at this random girl's pictures in my newsfeed, you know the girl that I have never met in real life who seems to have the perfect house, the perfect kids, the perfect skin, and, but of course, the perfect booty. Here is a NEWSFLASH we all know but seem to forget every time we scroll through the superficial newsfeeds, what people post on social media most of the time is NOT A REFLECTION OF THEIR REAL LIFE; it's their highlight reel. It's the best moments of their lives, carefully chosen, then sometimes edited to reflect the image they want the world to see. It's edited and FAKE. It's a manipulation of perception. I am sitting here in need of a shower, about four days at the spa, and comparing myself to the professional photos some girl, I don't really even know, posted last night, trying to convince the world that she has found the secret equation to achieve perfection. UGH! I am over it. Let's just take a moment and acknowledge the one-dimensional world we live in, now take it a step farther, let's choose to stop participating in the fraud and can we just be real, authentic, vulnerable even?

Can you imagine going through your entire life and never feeling beautiful? Never genuinely embracing the beauty within your soul, the beauty that is radiating from the inside out, penetrating the skin in which we are wrapped? I have met men and women as I have traveled to countries all over the globe and we all have one thing in common; we all have that dreadful list we use to tally all of our flaws- I call it the pretty tragic list. You know the list that I am talking about, the list of things that we HATE about our bodies and would change in an instant if we could. I have sat and had conversations with some of the most beautiful, successful, and well-educated people on this entire planet and still the longer we talk, the more the list rears its ugly head, hiding in our words as we reveal our hidden insecurities.

Beauty is an everyday struggle, both internally and externally, for everyone, especially women. Media, celebrities, Instagram, Photoshop, selfie filters, have all set such a ridiculously high standard of beauty which we allow to set the internal expectation for ourselves. We are our own worst critics, terrorizing our self-esteem every time we look into the mirror, hit repeat on the record player playing in our minds, keeping the pretty tragic list replaying line by line as we sit and stare at our flawed bodies.

Perfection is an illusion that we have all bought into. It can literally become an obsession to look and feel perfect. An obsession that leaves us feeling disappointed and empty. We strive for the perfect hair, eyebrows, eye color, cheeks, lips, hips, stomach, arms, butts, thighs, legs, practically every feature on our bodies, thinking somehow we can obtain this thing that we cling to, you know, the idea of the perfect body. I can look back at pictures of myself today from different time periods in my life and see the beauty I possessed, the body I would give anything to have today, well, minus how skinny I was, and yet at the moment, years ago when those photographs were taken, I felt ugly, undesirable, and gross.

The opinions of others can, and most likely will, change the way a person feels about themselves. The words from parent, friends, family members, and sometimes even strangers can become the fuel their inner critic uses to drown out every other voice. This is why we have to be so mindful of the things we speak over children. Most of the time, we are completely unaware of the impact a simple comment or joke can have on someone's life. Our words can intensify adult insecurities let alone a child's. Speak life and love over every child in your life. Adults carry around baggage from their childhood filled with negative comments by well-meaning adults. If they don't heal from the wounds of their childhood, they might grow up and bleed all over everyone, creating another generation of wounded people. So many of my insecurities stemmed from things I internalized as a child. I had to learn how to shift my mindset so I could understand I was beautiful, internally and externally. It didn't matter if everyone told me how pretty or beautiful I was; I had to learn to believe it for myself.

When I was younger, there were so many things I loathed about my body. My obsession with my weight and my big lips started at ten or eleven years old. I felt like it was the first thing that everyone noticed. It seemed like everyone found a way to point out how big my lips were or how skinny I was, even in casual conversations. I felt like my lips were the only things that anyone could see on me and something everyone thought was disgusting. In sixth grade, this girl had all of these lipsticks and glosses, every shade you could imagine. She was taking the girls one by one and trying the shades she felt would accentuate each girl's features. One by one, each girl lined up to be made beautiful. The girl that had all the products that made her perfect, the one each one of us longed to be. Excitement filled my body at first. I wanted to fit in, to be one of them, the beautiful ones. My excitement was quickly replaced with fear and anxiety layered between self-consciousness. My lips seemed triple the size of everyone else's in my class. Would they laugh at me? Would they point out my gigantic lips? Finally, it was my turn. I smiled, hopeful. I chose the lipstick I wanted, although more than the lipstick, I desperately wanted her approval. "Oh my gosh, Chanel, your lips are huge. You will use the entire stick for those lips!" I was mortified. All my fears and insecurities were true. After all the girls giggled, she added, "Why ARE your lips so big?" Crushed. I was humiliated, ashamed, I wanted to crawl away and die. Even though on the inside I was crying, I refused to let her win, to let them see me hurt. I allowed my heart to get hard, rose up and smacked the lipstick out of her hand and gave her the middle finger and just walked away, with attitude. Just kidding, that's what I wish I would have done! I just put my head down and softly said, "You don't have to use your lipstick on me," and I walked away.

My huge lips were not the only thing that made it onto my pretty tragic list. I felt like I had three rows of teeth. The crookedness of my bottom row and the way they were misaligned to the front row drove me insane. The top ones were just too big, crooked, and too ugly. My shoulders were next on the list. In my mind, my shoulders were masculine and built for a football player I felt, not for a small framed female. I refused to wear spaghetti strap tops.

I remember my teenage years, which was the most awkward stage of my life. My mother purchased some clothes for me. I was so excited. I mean, really, who doesn't love a new... ANYTHING! I was trying on all the jeans, of course, they fit me like boyfriend jeans which is great now but who wants to look like they are in boyfriend jeans at fourteen. I wanted form fitting clothes, but clothes that would fit a form that I didn't really possess. My mother absolutely loved them, I mean, of course she did. Why would she want her soon to be teenage daughter wearing skin-tight jeans? Who would want that? ME!!! I want fitted clothes. Strike that; I needed fitted clothes. I might have been young, but I knew what I needed to compete in this world. Next, I pull out what I thought was an undershirt because I just knew that there was no way she bought a spaghetti strap top for me. Reluctantly, I tried it on. I should add here for those of you that do not know me personally, my face tells on me. I mean, I have one of those faces that will not hide what I am feeling and thinking, even though I try. I know that the devastation I felt when I saw my arms was written all over my face for my mom to see. She may have bought me this cute spaghetti strap shirt to wear on its own, but as we both stared at this little shirt on my boyish frame, we both knew that it was most definitely an UNDERSHIRT for Chanel!

I have always been super-skinny, but I desperately wanted curves like the other beautiful women I would see. My long, thin frame made the body type I craved for impossible. I was called, "Olive Oil" from Popeye, "light pole," "stick figure," "skinny minny," "mawga," the list goes on and on. In school, it seemed as if all the other girls around me grew voluptuous breast, butts, and thighs overnight. How was I supposed to compete? I would wake up every morning, running my hands over my body as if to check to see if today was my turn.

One day, it happened. Change. I wanted to scream... FINALLY!!! My overnight growth seemed like a miracle to me but the change wasn't enough for anyone else to notice. I actually had some breasts. My new friends may have only been the size of niblets but they were there nonetheless. Then my jeans started to fit me differently. I had a butt. My curves were still small, but they were there, and I loved them. I no longer looked like a ten-year-old boy with big lips. My new curves came just in time for high school! I still had my pretty tragic list. I wanted smaller lips and braces for my teeth; I wanted to be a little thicker, with more curves; I wanted my hair to be a bit longer and straight; I wanted to change my name to Jasmine. I believed if I had all of those things and was able to have a new name, I would FEEL beautiful.

We are never satisfied.

The first time I felt beautiful was my high school prom. I was seventeen years old. My dress was beautiful. It was a plush pink with sequins; it sparkled and glistened in all the right places. It had a short train, and the low-cut back of my dress was to die for. My hair was twisted up into the perfect bun. I had my heels on that made me feel older, sexy even. I looked in the mirror and absolutely loved everything I saw. Years of insecurities melted away when I looked at the image reflecting back to me in the mirror. The dress was a perfect fit. I felt flawless. The only makeup I had on was a colored lip gloss. I felt like a princess. My prom was one of the best nights of my life. I didn't even have a date; I went with a group of friends. We had the full prom experience complete with the hummer limo, pictures galore, and lots of laughter. I felt beautiful. I received so many compliments from everyone; I know that I was glowing.

The beauty people were reacting to was the beauty that I felt radiating through my body. It wasn't just my physical appearance that changed. Although, I did clean up nicely. It was the way that I saw myself. The moment I realized how beautiful I was, I began to glow. People noticed and had to compliment me. I danced the night away; it felt like I was growing and blossoming into a young woman. All of the insecurities and flaws I had no longer existed.

I felt liberated.

Free.

Another time I felt beautiful was relatively recent. I booked a photo-shoot with Creative Elements photography. The entire week, I was so scared; anxiety took over. I was listening to that same old record. The lies I believed in my childhood about my physical appearance crept back in. They felt familiar, like they had never really gone away-just laid dormant waiting for the right time to remind me of all the ways I failed to measure up. I am my own worst critic. The negative thoughts swirled about the photo-shoot in my mind. I must have canceled the photo-shoot at least seventy times. I thought I would look ridiculous. I wouldn't get any great shots. I'm not pretty enough. My pretty tragic list played on repeat at the loudest setting. I felt hideous. I didn't know how I was going to find time to do my hair, my nails, let alone find the perfect outfit.

I took a breath. I centered myself. I created space to realign with the person I choose to be. I made the time and the day before to get my hair and nails done. I spent the time to find just the right outfits. The day of the shoot, I got my makeup professionally done. I looked flawless. Fierce.

I became obsessed with how beautiful I looked and felt. Now all I want to do is have photo-shoots. How did I not know this beautiful woman was living inside of me? And how can I help her resurface? I didn't want to take my makeup off, ever. I wanted to stalk the woman who did my makeup. I mean not really, but I would have loved for her to move in with me just to do my makeup every day. I was crying on the inside because of how beautiful I felt. I was floating on air. I felt confident and unstoppable, like super-wonder woman. We started shooting; the pictures were flawless, and that was all me. The photographer was fantastic, but he didn't even have to edit the photographs. For the first time, I felt like one of the girls in the magazines. The ones I had wished I had looked like my entire life. Suddenly, I was able to imagine myself on the cover of magazines. I was just as beautiful as the women I had worshipped in the past. I allowed myself to see what the rest of the world saw. I felt beautiful.

As perfect as the women and men we idolize may seem, like us, they are all flawed. We must learn how to accept and even appreciate our flaws. We can change the way we look, but it will not change the way we feel inside. We have to reach inward and align with our internal beauty. The way we feel on the inside can dictate the way we appear on the outside. Many people are dealing with such internal turmoil that no matter how beautiful they may look to us, all they see is their own pretty tragic list. There is no such thing as perfect, especially when measuring beauty. Perfection is a form of self-sabotaging idolism rooted in fear. It is a way to mask or distract ourselves from dealing with, or feeling, what we truly are experiencing within. True confidence is knowing who you are and accepting yourself, while embracing your flaws and owning your beauty. Not the faking until you make it or editing your photos to the point your own family can't recognize you. When you are aligned with your confidence, you are unfazed by the insecurities you once felt and are no longer triggered by the other beauty within the room. When you find yourself aligned to the kind of confidence you can only find from the inside, you will be at peace and truly love yourself.

I can look at my pretty tragic list every day, adding to it even, naming every way I would like to change; but I think, even if I had a magic wand that could magically wave away everything on the list, I would still be able to find something to add to it. My inner- critic can find the flaws in anything. I will never align with my internal beauty until I shut down my inner-critic and embrace myself fully. It doesn't matter what I reflect to the world if I don't accept myself and love myself.

Begin to silence your inner-critic and align with your internal beauty. Stop comparing yourself to the photoshopped versions of people you see online. Align yourself to your internal beauty, accepting, and loving everything about the beautiful person you are. You are beautiful. You are strong. You are phenomenal.

"Unpretty"

I wish I could tie you up in my shoes,
Make you feel unpretty too.
I was told I was beautiful,
But what does that mean to you?
Look into the mirror; who's inside there?
The one with the long hair,
Same old me again, today.

My outsides look cool,
My insides are blue.
Every time I think I'm through,
It's because of you.
I've tried different ways
But it's all the same.
At the end of the day,
I have myself to blame.
I'm just trippin'.

You can buy your hair if it won't grow,
You can fix your nose if he says so,
You can buy all the make up
That M.A.C. can make,
But if you can't look inside you
Find out 'who am I'

To be in the position that make 'me' feel
So damn unpretty,

I'll make you feel unpretty too.

Artist: TLC
Album: Fanmail, 1999
Record Label: LaFace Records LLC

4

Love Thy Self

You yourself, as much as anybody in the entire universe deserves your love and affection.
-Buddha

We don't understand the turmoil a child or adult is suffering internally. When I was eighteen years old, I attempted to commit suicide. I was depressed and felt all alone. I was overwhelmed with insecurities and covered with a blanket of shame. I felt like I was in a constant state of turmoil and I just wanted to be free from the self-inflicted torture I was going through. I had stepped so far into the darkness I could no longer see light anywhere. In a weak moment, I gave into the darkness and decided to end it all.

I struggled with insecurities through all of my childhood. When I was ten years old, I experienced trauma which changed everything about me. My innocence was stolen from me and no one knew. I was being abused and was too afraid to say anything to anyone. I didn't know what to do. I didn't understand how to respond or how to keep myself safe. I felt like it was my fault and that people might be mad if they found out. Once, I decided I was going to tell someone, anyone, because I just couldn't take it anymore. Then my ten-year-old self thought about my mom and how it would impact her, and I just couldn't do it. I didn't want to cause my mom any stress or pain; so I buried it all. I decided I needed to protect myself and handle the problem on my own. This is when I started to build the wall around my heart for protection and learned how to shove my feelings down. I smiled. I pretended everything was fine. I cried myself to sleep; slept with books behind my door as if it would. I lived in fear. I prayed night and day for my abusers' demise. I took every precaution to never be left in the same room with him again. He was persistent and would try to be around me anytime he could. I vowed he would never have the chance to touch me again. I did whatever it took to not be left in a room with him; smiling, the entire time, like nothing was wrong. He had passed away but the damage was already done. The impact to my life was already embedded. I felt relieved but not free.

    Despite my wonderful family and all the love they had for me, the secret was slowly eating away at my soul. My feelings bounced all over the place. One moment, I would be enraged and filled with hatred, the next moment, I would find myself crying uncontrollably with a deep feeling of sadness. I felt used, like a piece of trash. In the shower, I would scrub my skin trying to feel clean again, but I never could scrub hard enough. I felt weak; I believed

I was a victim and somehow, I deserved what happened to me. I was powerless.

I leaned into my perfectionist tendencies. I coped by throwing myself into my schoolwork and all of my extracurricular activities. My mom kept me very active; I was in dance classes, the Girl Scouts, and I played tennis. My family and I also took regular trips. I tried to distract myself with being busy. I covered up the pain with accomplishments. I was one of the smartest kids in school, yet every day, I hated myself a little more.

By the time I was fourteen, I was tired of wearing the mask. My smile felt too heavy. Depression set in. I began to have suicidal thoughts multiple times a day. I would daydream of different ways I could kill myself. I couldn't swallow pills, so maybe I could crush them and/or let them dissolve in my mouth. I visualized jumping out the second-floor window, but I was afraid I would just hurt myself. I didn't know how to hang myself, but I would still look up to see if I thought the light fixture could hold my weight in every room I entered. Externally, everything looked perfect, but I was deteriorating on the inside.

Until I was seventeen, I didn't realize how low my self-esteem had become. I self-sabotaged when things were going well and I set myself up for failure anytime I tried anything new. I was unaware of this, of course, I couldn't see how I was playing a part in my life falling apart. I allowed my fear and insecurities to become my guides, and my guides fueled my feelings of unworthiness. I thought I was in love, but I didn't understand I couldn't love anyone if I didn't first love myself. This relationship served as a mirror, forcing me to see how I really felt about myself. Brokenness attracts brokenness. Until you heal, you will only attract more brokenness in your life. It only took a few months for our relationship to become abusive. At first, I was just being controlled, manipulated, and told how awful I was on a regular basis. Soon, the abuse shifted from emotional to physical abuse. I stayed because I didn't think I deserved anything better. I felt like a piece of trash; why would I be treated any better?

The lowest point in my life began when I decided to be vulnerable and reveal my secret. Scared, I found the words, and I shared the story of my abuse for the very first time. The next day, he took my secret and humiliated me. In an effort to make me even smaller, he spewed vile accusations at me, saying I asked for it, liked it even. I was devastated. Here was this man who I shouldn't have ever trusted, but he was the one I chose to share my story with, he was the one that said he loved me and I felt like he needed to know. I opened myself up to him and he crushed me. I decided I didn't want to live anymore. I couldn't exist in a world filled with untrustworthy, selfish, deceitful people.

The demons, who had permanently taken up residence in my mind, began to become too loud to be drown out. They reminded me that I had been defiled and was unworthy of love. I felt rejected and disgusting. I couldn't muster up the strength to continue to live and decided my suffering had to end. I found three large white pills and crushed them up as I could still not swallow even the smallest of pills. I had no idea what they were, and I didn't care. I chased them down with fourteen shots of alcohol. I was done; done with the world and all the torment I felt inside. At 11:42 AM, I passed out on the floor. My stepfather came home from work sometime after four. He nudged my leg and told me to move to the couch. He had no idea what I had done. I tried to make my way to the couch. The room was spinning and my head felt like it was about to explode. I came to a couple of times but couldn't move my body. My mother came in around 6:30 PM. She was on the phone telling someone, "She is fine; she's laying on the couch." She nudged me. "Chanel, Chanel, are you OK?" I was still out of it. She was able to wake me, but it wasn't making any sense. I tried to get up and make it to the bathroom. The room was spinning and I felt like I was going to puke. I thought I needed some air and tried to make my way outside. I barely made it to the corner. I went back to my house and told my mother I needed to go to the hospital. She had no idea I had tried to kill myself a few hours earlier. I started throwing up as soon as I got out of the car. She looked at me with the 'you better not be pregnant' look. Why is the first thought or question about pregnancy when a female is sick?

Once we made it to the ER, I started feeling worse. I broke down and told my mother what I had done. She looked at me completely mortified and then ran to the receptionist in a panic. I never understood the severity of it until nurses came to get me and placed me on a stretcher. I knew I had gone too far. In that moment, I realized how I was playing with my life. How I really felt about myself. How I must have really hated myself.

I was in a hospital room drinking liquid charcoal. The nurse thought adding ice would somehow improve the disgusting taste. It was black, extremely grainy, the texture was awful. I could feel it traveling down my throat; it felt like I was drinking sand. I thought to myself, 'I will never be here again.' I felt even more embarrassed, ashamed. I hurt the most important person to me, my mother.

I allowed my past to determine my present; it almost robbed me of my future. This was not the life changing moment it should have been, but it was a defining moment that exposed my suicidal thoughts. I realized I was playing with death and had a lot of deep rooted issues to deal with. I wish it would have been enough for me to understand I needed to leave the relationship I was in and begin to learn how to love myself, but I wasn't ready for that yet. I was still searching for the love I didn't have for myself.

The abusive nature of our relationship intensified. I was abused, violated, and humiliated on a regular basis. I didn't think I would make it out alive; fear engulfed my soul. One day, I caught a glimpse of myself in the mirror and I didn't recognize myself; my face was swollen, and there was blood dripping from my busted lip. Who was this woman? How did she get here?

I was broken; inside and out. Even though I was embarrassed, I had to make the decision to pick myself up and chose to learn how to love myself. It wasn't easy; none of it. My mind was bombarded with negative thoughts, but I knew if I didn't start learning how to be better, I would end up dead, either by the hands of an abusive man or by my own death wish. I found the courage. I took the first steps; sometimes all you need is just one gigantic baby step to change the rest of your life.

My past and the things that happened to me did not, could not, and would not define me any longer. My worth is not determined by anyone but myself. I had to see my worth. I had to learn to love myself.

I put in the work, and it was work. I had to work through forgiveness and deal with all the lies I believed about myself. I had to release all the judgements I made about myself. I had to learn how to be more compassionate towards myself. I had to stop thinking like a victim and see myself as a warrior. I had to accept myself as I am while working towards who I wanted to be. Almost my entire life, I had thought a certain way. I had been programmed to be the person that would stay in a relationship in which I was violated in every way imaginable. I had to put in the work and reprogram my mind. I had to learn a new way to act, think, and respond.

As a child, you do not have much control over your life. You don't get to choose your parents and you can't decide how or where you are going to live. As you grow older, you can make the choice and do not let your circumstances determine who you are destined to be in this world. I had to make a powerful decision to rise up from my circumstance. I had to choose me. I had to believe that I am important. I am worthy of love. I am courageous. I am a warrior. I am beautiful. I deserve to be loved properly. I deserve happiness. My past does not define me. I am destined for greatness.

You have to train your brain by thinking and speaking positively, and use affirmations to help you believe things you may not feel yet. You have to think it, say it, write it, and read it, over and over, until you have trained yourself to embody and accept these words as your truth.

Every decision I made, even down to the people I surrounded myself with, was a direct reflection of how I felt inside. Everything serves as a mirror. Most aren't willing to even start the journey of self-love because it is one of the hardest roads to travel. You have to look at yourself and expose who you have been to yourself. You have to inspect the root of the issue and understand the why and the how. It's an uncomfortable process. Most people would prefer to mask their pain with material things, job titles, a fake smile, with having a million friends, or with partying all night. It's easier to hide behind a mask than deal with the hurt you have been through. I went on a vicious cycle so I didn't have to look in the mirror, but one day, I decided enough was enough. I realized it starts with me. I needed and wanted a change in my life. I could no longer wait for someone else to save me… I had to do it for myself.

The real difficulty is to overcome how you think of yourself.
-Maya Angelou

This is where the journey of self-love began. It can be an everyday struggle. As you are changing and evolving, others around you are remaining the same. They have been comfortable with the person you have been since they have known you. The way you have allowed them to treat you; to take advantage. The way you allowed them to walk all over you and not even consider your feelings. The way you have accepted what they want to give you versus what you deserve. The way you accepted being under paid. The way you accepted being mistreated. You will lose a lot of people on the journey of self-love. It will expose those who really don't have genuine intentions. Those who truly aren't your friends or even a romantic partner. When you are setting boundaries and are saying "No," most won't like it. They enjoyed the old you- when you paid for everything, let them do as they pleased, and let them take what they wanted. However, those who are in your corner will celebrate your changes. They will be your biggest cheerleader. Those are the people you need to bring in closer. Don't be afraid to lose anyone who isn't meant to be on your new journey. They will only hold you back and keep you stuck. Focus on yourself. Love yourself and the right people will come along.

    We all want love from our friendships, families, and partners. Most of us want a partner, someone to share our lives with. We want someone that will show up for us in every way; someone who makes us feel important and validated. We want passion and a best friend. We want someone to value and treat us special, someone that can make us feel as if we are the only ones in the world.

    For so long, I would dream of being in love and having someone save me from my misery. I looked for validation from other people. Especially from the opposite sex; it felt amazing to be wanted, admired, and adored. Especially when your self-esteem is at an all-time low. You look for material things and people to add value to your worth. I am a firm believer that people are sent to either make you or break you. Sometimes, we chase after people that aren't meant for us and that is all tied to how we view our worth. We settle and accept the crap because we don't want to be alone. We don't truly feel good about ourselves. A beautiful man or woman just makes you feel a little bit better about yourself. The mere fact that they are even entertaining the idea of liking you, let alone being with you, makes you feel like you are the best thing in the world. We accept the scraps on a platter because it's better than nothing. We accept the mistreatment by lack of attention and fulfillment of our basic needs emotionally, mentally, and physically. Physically is more than just sex. You can be physically satisfied sexually but not with the time the individual is investing in you and being present in your life.

As I have already stated, we all want love, but our desire to be connected to someone doesn't give us a reason to settle. If a person is not on your level with their time, energy, love, attention, finances, they will most likely not be able to connect with you in a way that will fulfill you. When two people want different things or aren't on the same level in some way, it creates tension in their relationship and you might need to let them go. You want a partner, not just a lover. A partner is someone who will have your back, fight for you, and cheer for you. If you continually settle for less, then you might miss the one meant for you. For so long, I accepted less than; my settling was tied to my self-worth. I am in a place now where I will no longer beg or try to force anyone to provide the basic requirements of being in a relationship. The difference? I know my worth. I will no longer settle for scraps; I found my throne and I deserve the entire banquet.

This is tied to our careers as well. We all need money and have financial responsibilities. For so long, I accepted less pay and poor treatment by my bosses and co-workers. I was trained to be thankful I had a job. I felt undervalued and unappreciated. I got fed up. I was doing the same job as others for a fraction of the pay. This is no longer an option for me. I am well aware of the value I bring to the table. I know my assets and my worth. If a person, even your boss, doesn't treat you the way you deserve, #thankyounext. If you aren't paid, treated, or valued the way you deserve, #thankyounext. The time of being undervalued, mistreated, unappreciated, ignored, ghosted, unacknowledged ends today!

Remember, the way the world treats you is a reflection of the way you value yourself. The world responds to what you allow. Know your worth and value. Love yourself so much that the world will have no other choice but to love you.

"Beautiful"

Every day is so wonderful,
Then suddenly it's hard to breathe,
Now and then, I get insecure
From all the pain; I'm so ashamed.

I am beautiful no matter what they say.
Words can't bring me down.
I am beautiful in every single way.
Yes, words can't bring me down...
So don't you bring me down today.

To all your friends, you're delirious,
So consumed in all your doom,
Trying hard to fill the emptiness,
The pieces gone, left the puzzle undone...
Is that the way it is?

We're the song inside the tune,
Full of beautiful mistakes.
And everywhere we go,
The sun will always shine.
And tomorrow, we might wake on the other side.

Artist: Christina Aguilera
Album: Stripped, 2002
Record Label: Sony Music Entertainment

5
Purgatory

Think of your mind, your emotions, and your spirit as the ultimate garden. The way to ensure a bountiful, nourishing harvest is to plant seeds like love, warmth, and appreciation, instead of seeds like disappointment, anger, and fear.
-Tony Robbins

Purgatory is thought to be a place where someone is stuck. It's a holding place for the in between. In the past, I have been trapped in a self-made purgatory. I knew exactly where I wanted to go and who I wanted to be, but I was caught in a state of confusion. It was like I was on a private island, barely able to see the promise land off in the distance. There I was, stuck. I knew I didn't belong on the island, but I couldn't figure out how to get to the mainland; I had no boat, no bridge, no airplane, and no resources. I just sat there waiting, hoping to be rescued even though I knew deep down I was the only one that could save me.

A little over four years ago, I took the brave steps and dove into my journey of healing and self-discovery. It's been a long, hard road filled with ups, downs, and surprise twists and turns. I started the process so I could understand how to align with the dream I have for my life with my career, but I quickly realized I couldn't align with my future until I healed from my past. I have learned so much about myself, lessons I will always keep with me. I slowly began to transform into a new person. I still have more learning and growing to do, as we all do, but I could have never left my purgatory without the healing process.

When I started the process, I looked successful; I was accomplishing things, traveling the world, increasing my salary, feeling good, and looking good. I looked like I had it all together, but I was unsatisfied. To the world, it looked like I was living my best life on my own private island; to me, it felt more like I was trapped, stuck in the middle of the ocean on a small island with nothing but a coconut tree - oh, how I hate coconut. I had to stay here, in my purgatory, until I learned the lessons and did the work, even when I was frustrated. I had to understand there were no short cuts; I had to dig in and do the work, all of it.

What does purgatory look like? What does it feel like? It feels like being stuck between who I have been all my life, who I need to be, and who I want to be. Being stuck between what I deserve versus what I settle for; between comfortability and discomfort; between being taken advantage of versus setting healthy boundaries. I was tired of being mistreated, being taken advantage of, and having the life sucked out of me by energy vampires. I was tired of accepting the scraps people gave me. I was tired of the way I allowed people to treat me. Most of all, I was tired of how I treated myself. The lack of self-care took a toll on my physical body and my emotional health. I didn't understand myself worth, how valuable I was. I didn't understand the gifts I had been blessed with or that I was POWERFUL. For so long, I felt minuscule and acted as such for so many years. I accepted crappy salaries, crappy deals and relationships. I self-sabotaged my life because I didn't understand I was worthy to live out my wildest dreams. I was worthy to have love, real love, unconditional love. I was worthy of abundance and success. For the first time in my entire life, I chose me. Now, I know who I want to be; I have no confusion about that. I understand my value and worth. I no longer settle for scraps- I demand the entire buffet.

  Are you living in a state of purgatory? Are you on an island with no bridge or boat? Are you ready to leap and be on your journey? If so, you have to be done with letting yourself down. You must stop putting everyone else before your needs. It's time to care for yourself; mind, body, soul, and spirit. Feel your feelings, even the ones you perceive to be bad or unhealthy. It's okay to feel down and sad but don't allow it to engulf you; you're not allowed to stay on the island of self- pity. It starts with taking small steps, do one brave thing at a time. For weeks, I was stranded on the island, buried deep within a pit. It felt like I was never going to be able to pull myself out. I had become so good at fixing myself, just give me five minutes and I would be good. I knew how to shake off the feelings and slap on a fake smile, laugh a little, maybe even tell a joke. No one would ever know moments before I was in full breakdown mode hiding in the bathroom stall. This time was different. Despite my ability to shake things off, I was unable to mask my feelings. No more hiding.

    I had to go into a hibernation, a protective cocoon in order to be in a safe enough space to do the work. In the cocoon, I began to sift through all of my feelings- there were so many. I had shoved my feelings down for so long that once they started surfacing, I couldn't turn them off. I had look at each one, identify what they were, and work through each one of them. I had to get the tools I needed so I could climb out of the pit and get off the island.

    There are so many people counting on me to pursue my dreams and achieve my goals, but most of all, I am counting on myself. I had to do this for me. Even when I was living on my island, stuck in purgatory, I knew I was there for a reason. I needed this time in order to learn and grow. It was the place for me to prepare myself for the next season.

    The island was created to separate myself from everyone and everything. At first, it was for my sorrow, my disappointment, and my pain, but it became the place I would drift to in my mind to find solitude and rest. A place without drama or takers. I needed a place to escape from being taken advantage of. A place absent of people that drained me emotionally, physically, and financially. I needed my own island. A place to meet myself. I had to make the shift in my mind to understand that purgatory island wasn't meant to be a place I permanently lived or a place to drown in sorrow. It was a place for me to rebuild myself and my life. Once I made the shift and understood, I controlled purgatory. I was able to transform into the person I was supposed to be. It brought clarity and direction. Once I climbed out of the pit of despair, it was my sanctuary. A place I created to distance myself from the cycles of dysfunction I created, or at least allowed, in all my relationships. It was my landing pad when I crashed.

    My purgatory was the place I learned how to practice self-care, take care of my body, and my emotional health. It was also the place where I learned about boundaries and how to implement them. It was also the place where I slowly learned how to love the person I was, am, and will become. I learned to see my value and worth. I realized my need for unconditional love and slowly opened myself up to receive it. I forgave myself. I let go of the judgements I made about where I should be by now and accepted myself as I was at the moment. I took my power back. I stopped being a victim and took responsibility for every area of my life. I understood life was not a series of things happening to me but a series of choices I made or didn't make. I learned to stop settling and demand more for myself. I realized my worth and aligned with the truth- I am worthy to have an abundant life, filled with unconditional love, joy, and peace.

I was on that island for four long years, sifting through all the hurt, pain, trauma, disappointment, and regret. I had to choose to show up for myself, every day. Once I stopped searching for a way off the island, I gave into the lessons it had to offer me. Over time, I noticed the promise land wasn't as far away as I thought. The more I healed and began to love myself, the more I could see a small sliver of land stretching toward me.

Finally, I could see clearly. I knew my worth and my value. I could see the land was close enough; if I was brave, I could jump in and swim my way into the promise land. That's when fear set in. I had become comfortable in my self-made purgatory; it was familiar and felt safe. I didn't know what was in the water, how long it would take me to get to the land, and what I might face on the way there. Was purgatory really so bad?

Part of my island, my safety net, was my career. I finally made it to the position I thought would bring me happiness. I had the title I longed for and the salary to go with it- well, a portion of the salary but that's a story for another time. I had made it but the title and salary didn't deliver what I thought it would. It didn't make me happy; I was not satisfied.

During my time on the island, I realized another passion; I understood who I was created to be. I had to let go of one world in order to make my way to the next. I couldn't carry the identity I created with me into the promise land. If I tried, I knew I would have drown.

One day, I found the courage, I took a deep breath, and I jumped in; which looked like pure craziness to the world around me. I walked away from a successful career to start my dream. I realized I had everything within me to leave my purgatory at any time; I just needed to believe in myself enough to do it.

I needed my safe place to heal and deal with myself. Once I was ready, that safe place started to feel as if it was holding me back from something more. I had to align with my worth so I could see the something more. I had to align with courage so I could go after it. I had to let go of fear and people pleasing so I could let go of my title, my career, and pursue my dream.

Once I put my toe in the water determined to leave behind my purgatory, fear tried to set in. I quickly told myself, "It's OK to be scared, do it anyway." I took another step; slowly, I kept going. When the water started to get deeper, I dove in and swam. In my mind, I kept repeating, "Chanel, you got this, you are a warrior!" It seemed like no time and my feet found solid ground. I had made it out of purgatory and into the promise land.

What purgatory are you in? What's your holding pattern?

Repeat after me, "I got this. I am a warrior. I have everything I need already. I am ready to leap." Now, confidently walk into your promise land.

"Freedom"

I'm telling these tears, "Gonna fall away, fall away"
May the last one burn into flames.

Freedom! Freedom! I can't move.
Freedom, cut me loose!
Freedom! Freedom! Where are you?
'Cause I need freedom too!
I break chains all by myself;
Won't let my freedom rot in hell.
Hey! I'ma keep running
'Cause a winner don't quit on themselves.

Artist: Beyonce
Album: Lemonade, 2016
Record Label: Parkwood Entertainment LLC, Columbia Records

6

Patterns

Addiction, self-sabotage, procrastination, laziness, rage, chronic fatigue, and depression are all ways that we withhold our full participation in the program of life we are offered. When the conscious mind cannot find a reason to say no, **the** unconscious says no in its own way.

-Charles Eisenstein

Have you ever woken up and realized you're just fed up and exhausted with yourself? Tired of going around the same circle. Paralyzed by the vicious cycle wreaking havoc in your life. Confused on why you continuously self-sabotage and make the same mistakes over and over, and again. We are creatures of habit. We are attracted to patterns, things that feel familiar. Patterns help us feel comfortable. Unhealthy patterns lie to us, convincing us we are on the right path. It feels easy. Even when, deep down, we know these patterns are keeping us from moving forward.

When you think of your enemy, our mind likes to picture this dark, gross, demonic entity seeking to destroy our lives. Or maybe you picture specific people that have caused you great harm in the past. Most of us have a hard time understanding who our worst enemy really is and where that enemy resides. What if I was to tell you your worse enemy is you- and dwells within your mind? Now don't get me wrong, you don't have to be your worse enemy. Once you heal and learn to break unhealthy cycles, you become your biggest support system but until then, you are the one that will set you back and lead you to what's familiar; repeating cycles in your life until you are completely wiped out and ready to throw in the towel.

Life has a way of allowing you to go through the same circumstances time after time, offering you a lesson. It is a gift. If you don't learn the lesson attached to the circumstance, it will repeat as a way to offer you another chance. This continues until you grasp the lesson within the circumstance. The people may change, the situation may even change, but the feelings will be the same until you learn how to move through them in a healthy way.

Through my journey of healing, I encountered some amazing people that helped me understand the power and danger in generational patterns. Our environment shapes us, especially as children. We learn patterns early in life and mimic whatever is presented to us as normal. When I was in my early twenties, I met a young man, just sixteen years old at the time; let's call him, Cash. I had met Cash through a mutual acquaintance. I was drawn to him because he didn't seem evil; he was funny, honest, and seemed very genuine. I had been in the projects near the neighborhood I resided at the park. At the age of thirteen, Cash was charged with attempted murder. Thirteen. Think about that for a moment. What were you doing at thirteen? When I was thirteen, I was dying to be promoted to a cadet in girl scouts, my biggest worry was finishing everything on time so I could get that badge; let's be honest, I wanted to finish it before everyone else because as we established earlier, I was an overachieving perfectionist. While I was working hard to achieve girl scout greatness, he was out trying to survive by any means necessary.

As I sat across from Cash, I saw a human being that fell victim to the generational cycle of violence and crime. Read that again, I didn't see a criminal; I saw a victim. Was he guilty? Yes. He was also a child who didn't understand anything beyond the system he was born into where survival was the only aspiration. He couldn't see past his circumstances. He inherited generational cycles that created a reality in which he had no hope. His normal involved gangs, violence, crime, murder, hatred, and tragedy. He was thirteen when sentenced to jail. Most thirteen-year-olds are in 7th or 8th grade, starting puberty, or wishing they would, listening to music, obsessed with clothes and trying to fit in. While he was a boy trying to prove he was a man. Not all cycles are created; some are inherited. Generational cycles are repeated until someone decides enough is enough. I hope Cash has learned from his past and has decided to put in the work to break the cycle for all the generations that follow or will follow him.

The patterns in your life can be self-created, but they can also be learned or even passed down through previous generations. My heart breaks when I see children who start out ten steps behind everyone else because of the family they were born into and the exposure to toxic environments they should have been protected from. When you begin to sift through your own cycles, you explore the possibility of generational patterns being present in your life. Take an inventory of your family and look for repeated behaviors that show up in multiple family members. Try to understand the root cause of these patterns and learn from them. Most importantly, decide they end. Make the conscious choice to pass on healthy patterns of growth and abundance.

There are several patterns within my family. It took me a while to recognize that some of the things I was battling were the same for many of my family members. It truly saddens my heart and my soul to see how many of us struggled with self-worth and sought external approval in hopes to fill a void on the inside. I wasn't the only one who settled, accepting less than we deserved, struggling relationally, and struggling financially; it's all a generational cycle. I had to make the decision that it ends with me. Our family deserves more; individually and as a unified collective.

While it's important to investigate cycles in your life and compare them to patterns you see throughout your family in order to pinpoint generational cycles, it's equally important to understand the source of most patterns in your life- you. You are the architect. You are the creator of chaos in your own life. Circumstances will stay on repeat until you take personal responsibility and find a way to grow through them instead of denying your role in them.

After I worked through the generational cycles in my family, it was time for me to deal with the self-made patterns that were holding me back from the life I desired. Once I decided to look at myself and heal from my past, I began to notice the repetitive nature of obstacles in my life. Before, I missed the familiarity in the struggles of my life. I couldn't see past the differences in each situation to notice the commonality in each event. It's like the light turned on; in an instant, I could see clearly the vicious cycles of my own making- self-sabotage, toxic relationship with money and people, misplaced trust, self-deprivation, self-destruction, and a long list of relationships in which I allowed people to take advantage of me.

Self-sabotage is simply defined as any action that interferes with, or blocks, your desired intent. I self-sabotaged everything; relationships, jobs, finances, my education. Self-sabotage can take on many forms. My go to destructive behaviors included: procrastination; demanding perfection from myself and others; wasting time, energy, and finances; failure to take responsibility; creating a negative narrative in every situation; ignoring my physical needs, including failure to rest; ignoring situations and letting them build until complete destruction is unavoidable.

I have self-sabotaged in so many ways. I had a tendency to spend impulsively; chasing worth through material things. My old pattern was to live beyond my means which then caused chaos in my life. I had no financial plan; I just did things without thinking through the long-term impact. I looked for instant gratification by spending money I didn't have yet. If I wanted to go on that trip, I did. If I wanted the bag, I bought it. I didn't understand the value of money nor my own worth. I needed material things to make me appear important, successful, and worthy. I shifted my mindset because I realized I was digging a hole with my finances

I could no longer continue with the destructive nature of the patterns I created around my finances. I wanted financial freedom. More importantly, I didn't want to pass these cycles to my children. I desired to show them how to be responsible and live with an abundant mindset. I had to breakup with the dysfunctional relationship with money and create a new, healthy relationship. I started by changing my mindset. I know I still have work to do and there is always more to learn, but my life changed the day I decided to shift my mindset and take responsibility for my financial freedom.

I didn't understand that my fear of failure, fear of success, and my self-worth were the root of my self-sabotaging mindset. I self-sabotaged by making unnecessary purchases, making impulse financial decisions. I self-sabotaged by not writing things down, not planning and keeping things in my mind or in view which led to missed opportunities. I self-sabotaged by creating and adding to my own chaos and dysfunction. I regularly created chaos in my life by knowing I needed to leave by a certain time so I could be on time, then waiting for the very last minute to get ready. Now I'm rushing, panicking, and freaking out because I might be late. Hello! My name is Chanel, and I am the creator of unnecessary chaos.

I created a cycle of sabotaging behaviors because in my core, I believed I was unworthy. I bought into the lie that I was not enough; I didn't measure up. I knew eventually, the lie would be exposed and everyone would find out the truth that I was not enough; so I blew things up before anyone else had the chance. Anytime things were good and my life seemed to be on track, I would get fidgety. I would be uncomfortable in my own skin. It felt too good to be true. I had to mess it up before the truth was found out and everything was taken away from me. I believed that people would eventually see me as the girl who didn't belong and demand I leave; so I would take matters in my own hands and blow everything up.

I couldn't change the pattern of self-sabotage until I got fed up with it and took responsibility for my part. Self-sabotage is still a struggle for me; it has by far been the hardest pattern for me to break. The biggest difference is, now I understand how self-sabotage looks and feels, which allows me to recognize when it's operating in my life. Awareness and understanding has empowered me with the ability to know what's happening. Once I realize it, I can shift it.

I spent my childhood trying to prove my worth through overachieving. As an adult, I continued with this pattern but the act felt increasingly more difficult to keep up. I would overextend myself when on the inside, I was screaming, "HELL NO." I was a workaholic. I honestly felt like everything I did had to be twice as good. I felt I didn't have the option to make mistakes or have a bad day. I had to be on point, have a plan for a problem that didn't exist yet, and always be at least fifteen steps ahead. Some of it was my own worth issue, but the other part was very real. Because I am a woman, especially because I am a black woman, there was little or often no room for error. I felt if I was just shy of perfect, there would be no room for anyone to say anything negative. If I was kind enough, smart enough, looked decent enough, knowledgeable, friendly, funny, dressed well, shared enough, was selfless, smiled at the right time, I would be enough. I was just shy of perfection and it didn't matter. Someone would still find something negative to say. Acting in such a way would only mask how I truly felt on the inside but when I was alone with myself, it was tumultuous. I was just so tired of all the patterns I was cycling through.

Let's talk about money for a moment. I have to imagine most of us would say that we were not taught the proper way to handle and manage money. Let me make something clear, I am not placing blame on our parents.

You can only teach what you know. My parents have always worked hard and done well for themselves. I am so proud of both of them. But the reality is, no one talks about money, especially when it's a struggle. I had no idea how quickly a mountain of debt could form from poor spending habits.

When I had my son, I wanted to provide him with everything. I got caught up in the idea I could create a life for him that was full of meaning by giving him everything; toys, clothes, electronics. I spent enormous amounts of money on a five-year-old's wardrobe that he would/could wear for about three months before outgrowing all he owned. What kindergartener needs an Xbox, iPad, and all the sneakers you could imagine? It was ridiculous.

What I didn't realize was I was trying to fill a void by providing him with material things. I felt tremendous amounts of guilt from being a single parent. I lived in a constant state of fear believing I would never be enough for him. On top of that, because I was a single parent, I worked two jobs to provide this lifestyle for him which compounded the guilt I felt. I would use material things to ease my guilt. All the things I worked so hard to give him may have provided momentary joy, but none of it was lasting- well, none of it besides the mountain of debt that just kept growing.

I developed a toxic relationship with money by buying into the illusion of looking successful versus being successful. I love nice things, all of them. Give me the designer labels, all the newest gadgets, the car, the house, a passport full of stamps, photo albums filled memories from extravagant vacations, and book all the appointments- hair, nails, massage, skincare, all of it. I thought these things represented success. I believed I deserved them; I worked all the time; I needed something to show for it.

Successful people don't overspend and they do not carry a balance on their credit cards. Jay-Z says, "If you can't buy it twice, you can't afford it!" I had to realize this truth the hard way. I am still paying things off from years of overspending. I had to make radical changes in my spending habit. I had to force myself to get real with my money situation, look at my debt, and analyze why I felt the need to always pick up the check, go on every trip, and acquire every new thing. I was using things to prove my worth. I wanted to show the world I was enough, that I was important, and I did so with a little plastic card. That plastic card was my best friend and my worst enemy at the same time.

I had to take responsibility for my spending habits and my finances. I had to teach myself how to spend wisely. I began to filter my purchases through the words of Jay-Z; if I can't afford to buy it twice, with cash, I can't afford it, and I won't buy it. I had to unlearn what I believed about money, debt, and how success looked. I had to deal with the generational portion of my issues with money and then take responsibility for the dysfunction I added to the mix. My desired intent is to set my children up for success, real success, and I can't do that by passing on to them a toxic relationship with money. For them to be successful, I have to be successful.

I am going to get really real with you now. While investigating the patterns causing mayhem in my life, one thing stood out above all others, a series of relationships in which I experienced acts of betrayal, abuse (mentally, emotionally, and physically), and a list of relationships (both romantic and friendships) that took advantage of me, using me in every sense of the word. I've talked about this more in depth in my Evolv-U series on YouTube and podcast. I trust people quickly, and my open, kind heart has gotten led to a lot of hurt. I try to assume the best in people and was unable to see when their motives were selfish. I was the giver and attracted takers in every area of my life;

friends, partners, and at work. My heart has been broken many times. Each time, I would try my best to Band-Aid the gapping wounds only to have it shattered again. I had to hit the bottom and got F E D -U P before I could deal with the hurt and the pain of this cycle.

Once I was fed up, I began to set boundaries that were not well received. I had to learn how to speak up for myself and stop giving to the point of depletion. I believed I was a victim. I felt like these things happened to me and were out of my control, but that wasn't the truth. I played a role in it all and I couldn't change the cycle until I understood that.

I began to distance myself from the unhealthy relationships in my life; I realized my responsibility, my part, in the dysfunction. I allowed- this is worth repeating; I allowed people to walk all over me; to take advantage of me; to betray me. I ignored every red flag, every gut check, and all the flashing neon signs telling me there was a snake in the grass. When people show you who they are, believe them. Common sense, right? Not for me; I gave people second, third, and forth chances, and I was let down every time.

There was a lesson I couldn't see in all the hurt and pain. I believed a lie about my worth. I attracted takers because I believed I wasn't worthy of anything better. Every time I was betrayed, used, and hurt had nothing to do with the people or the thing they did; it had everything to do with how I felt about myself and what I believed I deserved.

I accepted so many things from people. I never understood why it would keep happening or why people thought it was okay. It frustrated the hell out of me. Then one day, I had an epiphany. Because I believed I was unworthy, I attracted people that would treat me as so. I realized this was a "me issue" not a "them issue." If I didn't change, I would continue to attract the same thing. I decided I am enough; I am worthy of healthy relationships; I am capable of standing up for myself. I had to learn how to love boundaries, not walls. Instead of walling people out as a defense mechanism, I had to use clear communication to establish boundaries that protected both of us. Most importantly, I had to believe and own my worth.

Everything you go through has a lesson within it if you are open to see it. You can learn something about yourself from every person in your life. If someone triggers you, lean into it. Explore why they make you feel a certain way. Use every experience as an opportunity to grow. Today, I can look back on my hardest times and find gratitude for the lessons and the growth each moment brought with it. When you look at your life this way, you can become unstoppable, unbothered, and experience a level of peace that is untouchable. You may not be able to go back in time and remove your traumas or learned behaviors, but you can find the root, pull it up, and plant seeds to blossom into a new and evolved you.

7
Family Ties

"Families are the compass that guides us. They are the inspiration to reach great heights, and our comfort when we occasionally falter."
-Brad Henry

Family is having a tribe of people to love you unconditionally in spite of you and your shortcomings. Your tribe can be one person or fifty-two. Family is loving and supporting one another even when it's not easy to do so. Sometimes family is having tough love. It's being the best person and version you could be so that you may inspire the ones you love. My family has been the grounding force in my life, and they have been there for me through every heartbreak and victory. I don't know where I would be without them. They are my tribe, and my tribe loves hard. They show up, they support, and they interfere when necessary.

My family is a major part of who I am today. We are there for each other in real ways. It's more than just my mom and dad; I see some of my extended family at least two-three times a month. I am talking my mother, my father, my brother Andre, my sister Jaeda, aunt Noreen, uncle Claudious, aunt Nicola, grandpa John, grandma Bernice, and my nanny Carmen- who is really grandma but because of her intense hatred of the word, she insists on being called nanny, so nanny it is. Cousins, they make up an entire crew and I am proud they are my crew; Marcus, Dwayne, Danielle, Calvin, Chris, Dameel, Brittany,

Aleeyah, Daniel. These are the family members closest to me; they have been there my entire life. Even the family members I have that I don't see as often have played a critical role in shaping who I am; Kenneth, Daniel, BJ, Alex, Marlon, Malik, Paul, Aunty Marlene, Uncle Tony, Uncle Dennis aka Uncle Den Den. Stacy Ann is one of my inspirations. She can juggle it all; wife, mother, and a successful doctor!

From my birth until I was almost eighteen, I lived in a four-family home. Each floor was occupied by different family members including my grandparents, their children, and their children's children. We did everything together including house-parties, special gatherings, and lots of family dinners. All of our shared meals were filled with laughter, arguments, games, and drama. We even vacationed together. Even today, it's a mandatory obligation as a member of our family to attend Thanksgiving in Florida and our yearly family vacation. We travel together, work together, support each other, and spend time together whenever we can. Most people are astonished about the size and the closeness in our family, and I am shocked more families aren't like ours.

As much as I love our big, beautiful family, I am under no illusion that our family has reached any form of perfection. Like all families, we have our share of dysfunction and drama but through all the good, bad, and sometimes very ugly situations, we work through it and stick together. Even when some people are fighting and stop talking for a moment or two, at the end of the day, we show up for each other. If there is an issue, we side with family. Always. One minute we might be screaming at each other, but if someone comes for any one of us, we forget all about our fighting and join arms. It's us against them; every time.

My cousins were my first group of friends. There was a group of six of us- Marcus, Dwayne, Calvin, Danielle, Chris, and myself until the rest of the grandkids came, Dameel, Jessica, Andre, Brittany, Aleeyah, Jaeda, and Daniel. Then there was thirteen of us. We did EVERYTHING together. We went to the same schools until middle school, did the same group activities, went to camp together, and had lots of fights. We still hang out and spend a lot of time with each other. I love every single one of them. We have all grown up and have led our own separate lives but we always come together and we know we will always have each other's back.

When we were younger, we caused a ruckus in the house until about 3:30-4:30 pm on Monday through Friday, and on Saturdays until about 1:00pm because that was when Grandpa got home. To this day, I am scared of my grandpa at times. I have to remind myself that I'm a grown woman. He was always an authority figure to all of us. All he had to say was "Pack it in." We would all scurry to the couch and sit quietly, awaiting his instruction. He is the provider for our family; he took care of us all. He successfully started his own company and was able to support all of us. He is the head of our family. Although we feared him, we loved him and still do. He has a heart of gold. My grandma was just the kindest, sweetest, most nurturing person in the world. She too was an entrepreneur and ran her own child care business. We were her first babies. She was the absolute best and was so loved by all of us. My grandparents were both born in Jamaica. They made the long voyaged to England; my grandpa by boat and grandma by plane. I was quite shocked that my grandma flew on a plane. I thought it was like an Amelia Erhardt plane but no, it was a legitimate plane. They spent a number of years in England, had some children, four to be exact, my grandma already had six kids, and eventually made their way to New York City. I can't even see myself moving to New Jersey, let alone another country. It takes great courage and faith to take a risk like moving to another country, not once, but twice! I believe they taught us all to be brave and go after our dreams just by seeing how they lived their lives.

My parents are like superheroes. I know that God picked the best parents for me to have. They are wonderful, loving and supportive. They may have not been able to stay together, but their relationship issues never stood in the way of their love for me. They are super cool with each other. Again, some may think it is odd but because of this, they were able to co-parent so well and effortlessly. I knew I was supported, loved, and that I had two people that believed in me and were willing to fight for me. They didn't possess a lot of material wealth, but they sacrificed and made things work for us. They celebrated in all of my highs and they helped me pick up the pieces when I was at my lowest lows. My parents were young and had to learn how to be parents when they were still growing into adults. They had their own relationship and growth matters to tend to, but they always showed up for us. As a parent myself, I understand now the challenges they faced and the hard work it took to juggle all of their responsibilities. It's not easy being a parent; raising children is a challenge for even the most prepared. It's one of the hardest jobs there is; it's

24 hours a day, 7 days a week, 365 days a year- but it feels like even more than that somehow.

I would never blame any of my shortcomings on my parents. They did the absolute best job they could with the resources and knowledge they had. When your younger you swear you know everything, insert eye roll here; I was no different. Like so many teenagers and twenty-somethings, I actually made my life harder than it needed to be. For so long, I beat myself up because I felt I had let my parents down because of the poor life choices I made as a young adult. At a dark point in my life, my parents had to show me tough love and let me go. I completely understand their decisions now. As children, you don't know, and quite frankly, you don't care about how your parents make things happen; you just know you need them to. I decided to become rebellious at seventeen. It wasn't that I had become a rebel in a sense. I had someone in my life who wasn't the best for me. They had me emotionally and mentally wrapped around their finger. I was making poor decisions and was so engulfed with the idea of love. I fell completely off the path I was on. In life, people are sent as blessings or distractions. This person was a full-blown distraction. It didn't matter who gave me advice, who told me what I needed to do. I had to make the choice for myself. I didn't understand the amazing family I had and how much they truly loved and supported me. I was smothered and blinded by my own demons. When I needed them the most, they showed with open and extended arms.

It saddens my heart that there are so many children who haven't had the luxury of having two amazing parents or don't have parents at all. My parents have been my biggest cheerleaders. I owe them for all I have and for who I am. They show up for me in big ways, even still, today; recitals, honor roll ceremonies, graduations, prom, the birth of my children, events, trips, games, performances, all of it, they are there. Not only were they there physically, but they have also been my emotional support system. People might tell you that parenting ends at eighteen, when you are of legal age to be an adult- lies! I still, and always will, call my mommy and daddy when things are good, and especially when things are bad. I have needed them through my adult years as much as I did when I was a child; maybe even more. I love them with all of my heart and I thank them for being the most amazing parents to me, and grandparents to my children. I have made it my mission to be a great parent to my children, and be even better. My goal is to set the same standards and morals with my children and bring it to the next level.

I have two younger siblings, Andre and Jaeda. I am seven years older than Andre and sixteen years older than Jaeda. I am proud to be their sister. We all love and support one another. Their success is my success: Their happiness is my happiness. Andre taught me how to care, protect, and love someone younger than me. Jaeda taught me the necessities of being a mom. When my mother had Jaeda, I was sixteen and was old enough to help my mother out. I was already working part-time and I would help by buying Jaeda sneakers and clothes. I didn't realize my little purchases didn't even cover a measly 5% of the expenses related to having children until I had my own. I made her bottles, changed her diapers, and brought her to daycare. She was like my little baby. I still see her as one of mine; if I am doing something for my children, I try to include Jaeda.

Andre and I had a similar upbringing. We were never far apart; if Andre was there, I was either right next to him or just around the corner. He is such a great person; funny, kind, genuine, and selfless. He will soon graduate school and work in aviation. He has always worked and saved his money. My goal is to be more like Andre financially. I am always impressed with how he is able to manage his funds. Jaeda is the typical baby, you know the youngest that seems to be the most spoiled and able to get away with murder. I promise there is not one grain of salt about it- we love to joke about the way the world seems to revolve around Jaeda and we are just happy to be a part of it! It's hilarious to compare what she is able to get away with to our stricter upbringing. As much crap as we give her, let me be very clear, we all think she is phenomenal- and she is. She is an honor roll student who is somehow able to keep her grades up and still be a rockstar athlete; excelling in track, lacrosse, and dance. She is independent and started a part-time job as soon as she could get her working permit. I am proud of who each of them are within our family and in this world.

The family you are born with will be the family you have; unfortunately for some, you don't get the option to choose who your family will be. I am not unfortunate; I wouldn't trade my family for the world. We aren't perfect by far, but I wouldn't be the person I am today without my family. The level of support, the experiences, the life we have lived has set us up the best we can. They exposed me to so much greatness and I have been able to extend all my lessons to my children.

My family values travel and shared experiences. I have passed that value system on to my children who have been blessed to get to travel the world. Both my children have traveled outside of the country and they both had their first flights under the age of one. It's imperative for my children to know there is so much more to this world than we can ever imagine; so much more than our current situations and environments; so much to do and see. If I can expose my children to new and innovative things, it's my responsibility as a parent to do so. As parents, we have a direct impact on our children's lives. I will do all I can to ensure they have an abundant life. There are some grown adults who haven't even left the country yet or even have a passport. You have to experience new things. This is the only way you grow and develop your mind. My children will understand boundaries but know there are no limits to the life you can live. We spend lots of time together. I show up and support them in any way I can. I wipe their tears and I am their biggest cheerleader – all of this is because of what I had growing up. I appreciate it all. We weren't the richest family, but we have always made things happen, even now.

There are usually experiences while you are growing up that one has to overcome. There isn't one family that is perfect; perfection doesn't exist no matter how badly we want to create it. Your family doesn't define who you are as an individual. There are things my family didn't know but I made the choice to go out and learn, and to make necessary changes. One lesson I had to learn was no one owes you anything. If you had traumatic family experiences, forgive and let go for your own growth and happiness. Your family and your past don't have to define who you are. I believe you have been put on this earth for a reason and all that you have experienced, and all you have overcome, is part of your purpose, because it is part of your story.

      Your family is part of the journey but they aren't your journey. As you learn and grow, this life is yours and only yours to live. Release yourself of your family's expectations; release yourself of your family's approval; release yourself of the way you may have been hurt; release yourself of the father or mother you didn't have; release yourself of the way your family may have treated you; release yourself from toxicity, dysfunction, and chaos. Just because they are your family doesn't mean you need subject yourself to being mistreated or hurt. Create healthy, loving boundaries and standards, live in your truth and in your happiness. No matter how big or small your family is, if they genuinely love and support you, they will understand and show up for you.

8

Lost Love

"Ever has it been that love knows not its own depth until the hour of separation"

-Kahlil Gibran

When I was ten years old, I lost someone I loved for the first time. Before that moment, death was something I never gave much thought to. My Uncle, Anthony Henry, who I knew as Uncle Junior tragically passed away with his nephew, O'Neil Munroe. They were at the beach, enjoying the sun, sand, and family when my cousin was caught in a riptide. My Uncle heroically went out to save him. My cousin had died on the scene, my uncle was in a coma and eventually passed, leaving behind three children.

I can remember the moment I heard the news like it just happened. I was in the bath when my mother came in distraught. I couldn't understand what she was trying to tell me at first but I knew it was bad. After she found her words, I learned of the horrific accident. It was a major blow to our family; Their death shattered our world.

The last time I spent with them was when we all drove to Florida on one of our family vacations to see my Uncle Junior. My cousins, O'Neil Marcus and Calvin, had stayed behind in Florida with my Uncle. We were back home in New York and getting settled in. My grandmother always had some event or trip planned for us and that day was no different. She had planned a bus trip for us. We went out to Hershey Park; it was a great day. We loved being with our Grandma and we always had fun; even if it was as simple as going with her on a Saturday morning to run her errands. Our day of fun ended with getting the tragic news of my Uncle's passing; all of our lives were changed drastically thereafter.

The impact this loss had on my family is unmeasurable. My Uncle's children were left fatherless. I can only imagine how this shifted their paths and shaped their lives. Sometimes, I sit and think about how things would be different if my uncle was still alive. As trauma often does, the hurt and pain his children, parents, and siblings suffered over the years potentially changed who they are and how they navigate through life.

I miss him.

One of my high school friends had passed away. It was sudden and unexpected; tragic like my Uncle's death. He was so kind, had such a great heart, and was one of the funniest people I knew. He was well liked and had a great group of friends. Soon after his birthday, he was stabbed by a person he had a personal relationship with. We were all in shock. Shaken, we mourned the loss of our friend and began to appreciate the fragile nature of life, as well as each other's friendships. Many of us struggled with the lost love we felt for our friend. He was, and still is, missed by many.

There aren't many loyal, supportive, selfless, genuine people in this world. When you find one, you cherish them. In my life, I have often surrounded myself with people who wanted to be around me for the benefit I could provide them. I allowed many to take advantage of me. There have been very few who have truly wanted the best for me, to succeed, and not spew their own insecurities or issues on me. One person who has had a great impact on my life was Karlene Dyer. She was a phenomenal woman and mother. Our relationship meant so much to me; I wrote a chapter about her in a book I co-authored about people who inspired us titled *Love, Mama*.

Even though I only knew her for a couple of years, she changed the trajectory of my life. She was funny, brutally honest, caring, loving, and nurturing. She had my back the same way I had hers. I knew she had my best interest at heart. We could be raw and open with each other. We both knew we could call or text each other anytime. I wanted to help her succeed in any way I could. She deserved it. She spent her entire life pouring into others; I recognized that and wanted to pour into her. I saw myself in her. Her heart was gold. If you played with her, she was a force to be reckoned with.

I was working as the General Manager of a hotel in NYC and it was one of the hotel partner's events. It was her first big event; she was so fired up, happy, and she was able to be a part of the experience. I got to witness her becoming a fierce woman of business. I knew she was on track to become the Director of Sales of her own property one day. We laughed and hung out like high school girls at the dance party. It was amazing. We were enjoying our time together so much that even though the party was ending, I didn't want to leave her. We were in Washington Heights; this was my first time hanging out in this area. I was not interested in staying in the area so we shared a cab home. We talked the entire ride, pouring our hearts out all the way to my house. She talked about work, her kids, her husband, her health, how she was feeling, her frustrations, her fears, her wants. EVERYTHING! When we pulled up to my house, I didn't want to go in. I had been gone almost 8 hours and my kids were inside. I had to go in, but I wanted to take the Lyft to the closest Fridays so we could just chat and hang out a little longer, but I didn't. I couldn't. I hugged her tight and told her I'm always here if she needed me. That was the last time I saw her alive. To this day, I still regret not going to Fridays.

A couple of weeks passed. One morning, I woke up to a text message saying Karlene had died; July 15th, 2018. I couldn't believe it. I was at a total loss for words. She had touched so many lives. She was finally finding herself and living her life. My heart broke for her husband and kids. She was the matriarch of her family. Everything she did was for them; they were her life. They too had now suffered from love lost.

The biggest loss I have ever suffered was the passing of my Grandma. She was the matriarch of our family and one of the best people I ever knew. She showered all of us with so much love, taking care of us all. She poured her heart and soul into her family. I lived with her from birth until I was in high school. We all lived in a four-family home. It was the best way to grow up. She was the best. She was a part of everything we did. She was always there for us. She helped us, cooked us meals, showed up when we needed her, and even when we thought we didn't.

She was in Florida with my grandpa when she passed. I happened to be in Fort Myers for the weekend and was the closest relative that could get there to support my Grandpa. I believe everything happens for a reason. I was actually supposed to be in Fort Myers in December.

The weekend I was supposed to leave, my job approached me with a task force opportunity in Atlanta. I had done task force many times with my company but only within New York City. It was the opportunity of a lifetime for my career. I was supposed to be in Fort Myers to launch my own business. I had to cancel all my plans last minute and head to Atlanta. The weekend was a great experience. I was born to help companies identify their strengths and weakness, while developing strategies to improve. As good as the weekend was for my career, something else was going on. I had to reschedule my trip to Fort Myers for January.

When I was at the airport waiting for my flight to Fort Myers, my mother called and said my grandma wasn't feeling well; she had been running a high fever. I asked her if I should change my flight to Orlando so I could take care of her. My mom encouraged me to continue with my trip, explaining that my aunt was looking into tickets to make her way down there. My Grandma had been in the hospital a few times but she was a fighter and always got better.

I flew to Fort Myers for a rewarding business trip. My entire career had led me to this point. After spending two days in Fort Myers, Maximum Evolution was ready to be launched into the world. After the website was polished,

I was ready- January 4th, 2018, my baby, Maximum Evolution, made its debut in this world. That night, my body was exhausted but my mind was restless. I should have been celebrating or, at the very least, resting, but my thoughts kept going back to my grandma. At first, I thought it was because I wanted her to see my new website and hear all that I had accomplished but somewhere deep inside, it seemed like there was something else pulling at my heart.

The weeks leading up to this trip were packed full of just about everything you could imagine. I had worked more hours than I could log in while I was in Atlanta for the task force. Christmas came with its own level of busyness. I had celebrated the New Year and then traveled to Fort Myers to finish the work with my team, to finish the launch of Maximum Evolution. I. Was. Tired. Exhausted. Yet, somehow restless. Knowing I couldn't function on another sleepless night, around midnight, I gave in and took a sleep aid.

I woke up at 7:36am with missed calls and hundreds of text from my family. Still today, the first thing I do in the morning is check my phone if I have several missed calls or texts; before I knew what they were about, my heart rate rose. My family was letting me know that my beloved grandma was not doing well. They were all up in New

York in a snowstorm. No flights were available, so they were planning to hop in cars and try to make the drive. I was in Fort Myers with my executive business coach doing an intensive in order to finish launching Maximum Evolution; we still had two more days to go. I called her to let her know what was going on and tell her I was trying to find transportation to Orlando. She told me to wait, came right away, and drove me all the way to Orlando. She stayed with me the whole time I was at the hospital, helping me make decisions and listening to instructions from the staff so we would know what needed to be done.

My grandma was already gone when we got there. I was about thirty minutes away when I got the call. On January 4th at 3:36 PM, my grandma passed. I felt my heart plummet to my stomach; I started shaking and felt like I might throw up. As we pulled up to the hospital and made our way to my grandma's room, I felt like I was having an out-of-body experience. I knew I was there, but none of it felt like it was happening to me. We made it to my grandma's room and a kind woman, who I had never met, was waiting for me. She asked me if I was ready. How could I be ready? My insides were screaming, "No! No! I'm not ready; what are you talking about?" but I felt my head nod yes.

I walked into the hospital room. If I close my eyes, I can still go back there and relive every second I spent in that room; I can taste the stale air, smell every chemical, hear every sound, and feel every feeling like it is happening right now. My grandpa was leaning over the love of his life, weeping and holding her hand. My grandma's body was still and peaceful.

I still hadn't fully digested what was happening. I kept running through details in my mind reminding myself- Chanel, you are in the hospital with your grandpa; your grandma just died; your family is all hours away; your grandpa needs you; your family needs you; Chanel, your grandma is dead; Chanel, you need to do something; your grandpa has to leave this room; Chanel, you are going to have to take your grandpa; Chanel, your grandma is dead; grandpa needs to go home; Chanel, wake up.

Suddenly, my body and mind caught up with each other and I realized what was going on. I began to sob, uncontrollably. Then I remembered the list I had been running through in my mind- my grandpa, I was here to help my grandpa. I pulled myself together. My grandpa didn't want to leave his wife. He knew this would forever be his last memory with her and he didn't want it to end. He knew when he walked out of that room, he was a widow. He was trying to be strong but he could not hide the pain in his eyes. After two hours, it was time; more than time, really. I placed my hand in my grandpas', our fingers interlaced. Together, we walked out of the room and into his new reality.

My grandma's death has been the biggest loss for our family. She had fought many battles. She had suffered for years from diabetes; even losing a leg in 2011. Her life was forever changed from it. Imagine being a strong, independent woman, the matriarch, cooking and cleaning, running your own daycare, being mobile as you please, then your health takes a turn and you become dependent and unhappy. The grandma I knew slowly begun to change. I understood it. I understood her pain, and her sadness. I wish I had the power to change it for her. I wish I could have been the person she had been to me my entire life. I made it my business to make sure we flew to see her in Florida; I didn't care how much money it was.

We traveled together often, as a family. The last vacation she had her leg was in Mexico, in 2011. The trip was a challenge because of her inability to walk but never the less, we were on a boat in Cancun travelling to Isla Mujeres. We all helped to push her wheelchair. We all worked together to make things easier for her. I remember driving a golf cart on the island with my kids and grandpa in tow; it was both fun and terrifying. I kept imagining me tipping the cart over and never hearing the end of it from my grandpa. He forgets NOTHING!

The last family vacation we were on all together was in 2014. We went to Jamaica for a family reunion. I remember it was like yesterday. We had an absolute blast. It was so great to have her there with us. It had been the first time she had left the country with us for a few years. It felt like old times to have our grandparents there with us. The food, the excursions, the family bonding, and all the laughing felt like home to us. It was everything I could have imagined it to be. My grandmother was a phenomenal person.

Her funeral was one of the saddest days of my life. I don't think I have ever cried so much. I was honored by giving a speech during the service. Inside, I was a hot mess as I was speaking about the life and loss of our grandma. As I stood in front of my entire family, I could see a glimpse of how many people's lives my grandma influenced. In the crowd, I could see her eyes, her smile, her nose, her hair; each person possessed a piece of her. I had my eyes fixed on my grandpa, the patriarch of our family. He sat tall trying to appear strong, which he is, but I knew on the inside, he was shattered. They had been in each other's lives for over fifty years; he would have to learn how to exist without her. He suffered lost love.

They say time heals all wounds, but I am not sure I believe that. Loss is loss; yes it gets easier with time but the ache will always be there. Since my grandma's passing, my sweet grandpa hasn't been able to sleep in their bed. Luckily, they have four bedroom so he was able to migrate into a new room. His life is forever changed by lost love.

As much as I miss her, part of me feels happy because she is free of pain and misery. She was suffering and struggling mentally, emotionally, and especially physically. My grandma was so independent; she had her own business, she was the matriarch of our family, she would cook every day, she would move how she wanted to and handled the business affairs of the family. She would get up on a Saturday morning and run the necessary errands. She lived in Florida for a couple of years alone, as my grandpa was running his business in NYC. Once her health took a turn, she wasn't able to be as independent as she once was. I know it was heart-breaking for her. She had to be taken care of and was bed ridden due to the loss of her leg and other health complications. I can only imagine how it impacted her. You battle with the person you once were versus who you are now. It is hard to accept if your life takes a turn for the worse; it doesn't matter how beautiful life may be around you. She was always a fighter. She overcame so many adversities throughout her life. She was so courageous and an overcomer. She was such a blessing to any and every one she crossed paths with. It is truly hard every day being without her. I know her mind, her heart, and her soul is at peace but I miss her being here every single day.

Life is fragile. Relationships are fragile. Our relationships have a great impact on our lives; they shape our values and hold up a mirror to our soul, revealing who we are. Do we take the time to think about the impact people have on us? Do we value our relationships while they are happening? Does it take a loss for us to realize the gifts we have? Does grief bring with it gratitude? Can we tap into that gratitude without experiencing the loss and learn to enjoy each other in the moment?

We all experience lost love through death and the ending of relationships. Each lost love shapes who we are. Sometimes lost love is unexpected and turns your life upside down, forcing you to muster up the strength to move forward. Other times, lost love comes in the form of moving on from a relationship that has run its course, allowing you the space to become something more. Regardless of the cause of the lost love, it's your job to forgive, let go of regret, mourn the loss of the relationship, learn the lessons offered, grow from the experience, and celebrate the impact the relationship had on you.

9

Motherly Love

"Phenomenal Woman"
MAYA ANGELOU

Pretty women wonder where my secret lies.
I'm not cute or built to suit a fashion model's size,
But when I start to tell them,
They think I'm telling lies.
I say,
It's in the reach of my arms,
The span of my hips,
The stride of my step,
The curl of my lips.
I'm a woman
Phenomenally.
Phenomenal woman,
That's me.

I walk into a room
Just as cool as you please,
And to a man,
The fellows stand or
Fall down on their knees.
Then they swarm around me,
A hive of honey bees.
I say,
It's the fire in my eyes,
And the flash of my teeth,
The swing in my waist,
And the joy in my feet.
I'm a woman
Phenomenally.

Phenomenal woman,

That's me.

Men themselves have wondered
What they see in me.
They try so much
But they can't touch
My inner mystery.
When I try to show them,
They say they still can't see.
I say,
It's in the arch of my back,
The sun of my smile,
The ride of my breasts,
The grace of my style.
I'm a woman
Phenomenally.
Phenomenal woman,
That's me.

Now you understand
Just why my head's not bowed.
I don't shout or jump about,
Or have to talk real loud.
When you see me passing,
It ought to make you proud.
I say,
It's in the click of my heels,
The bend of my hair,
the palm of my hand,
The need for my care.
'Cause I'm a woman
Phenomenally.
Phenomenal woman,
That's me.

There might not be a more true saying than, "A mother's work is never done." The challenges of motherhood never seem to end. Most people think the hardest part of motherhood is when your children are babies; but that's not really the truth. Each stage of motherhood holds within it its own challenges. Some moments take your breath away, and you are unable to understand how you could ever feel any more joy than you do in that very moment. Other moments make you question everything about your life and your sanity. Sometimes you go to bed exhausted, sad, victorious, defeated, confused, or the happiest person on earth. Sometimes you feel like you are the best mother in the universe and others you are secretly fearing the social worker someone has surly called on you. Motherhood is confusing but it is wonderful.

I take my hat off to anyone with three or more children; there are days when my two kids cause me want to rip off my wig. I don't know how people are able to manage more than two. I love my children but the lord knows sometimes when I hear "mommy", the hair on the back of my neck stands at attention and evokes the feeling of being completely overwhelmed. Even on the hardest days, you know the ones where you contemplate banging your head against a brick wall; I don't know where I would be if I didn't have my children.

I never knew how hard it was to be a mom because my mom made it look so easy. Now, I understand the trials and tribulations my mom went through. I can see the sacrifices she made for our family, at least in part; I don't think any of us can ever understand the full extent of what our mothers went through with us, but I have been able to appreciate so much more of what she has done for us. My mom; let me tell you about this woman. She is a phenomenal woman. She embodies the essence Maya Angelou describes in her famous poem- *Phenomenal Woman*. Even something as powerful as this beautiful power fails to describe the nature of my mother… there are no words that can combine to express her power as a woman and as a mother. Every day, my mother gives all she has to her children; she always has. She will make any sacrifice necessary to aide in our success and happiness. When I was younger, my mother was working full-time and decided to go back to school in order to better herself and all of our lives. I think I was about ten or eleven years old. She was determined to accomplish her goal of being a college graduate. Luckily, she had the support of the entire family. They would take care of us while she was at work and while she was in class. So many people don't have the same level of support as my mom did. She taught me perseverance, endurance, and strength. Watching her accomplish her dream was truly inspiring. I missed her while she was away but I knew it was a temporary sacrifice for a greater purpose. As a parent, you can feel guilty because you have to be away from your kids. Although I didn't fully understand what she was going through at the time, I can remember being so proud of her and how hard she was working. She has had to overcome so many adversities. Anytime life circumstances knocked her to her knees, she found a way to rise. When life pushed her, she pushed back. Any storm she faced, no matter how dark it might have been, she was able to see even the dimmest light and navigate to it. She is kind, yet feisty, just enough sass to keep you on your toes. She creates space for people to open up to her, accepting them in their rawest form. She is my safe place. The place where I can fall apart, be real, honest, and unfiltered. She has freely given me unconditional love my entire life, even when I was awful to her. She is my rock, my best friend, and my inspiration. One of the reasons I work so hard is because I hope to be able to take care of her and provide anything she needs. I want to add peace to her life and take away even just a fraction of some of the stress she feels. Watching her has helped me be the woman I am, and the mother I am to my children. I appreciate every lesson she has taught me and hope to leave even a fraction of the legacy she has already obtained.

When I was younger, I struggled with my self-worth. At the age of nineteen, I found out I was soon to be a mom myself. I was barely an adult and somehow, I was supposed to be responsible for another human life. I was clueless. I had no idea how much a baby would actually impact my life. Unemployed and without any plan, I gave birth to my son. He was so attached to me I couldn't do anything, even showering felt impossible at times. Even though it was hard, so hard, I mostly enjoyed each day; even the days filled with throw up, no sleep, and lots of tears. In some ways, it was the best times of my life, in other ways, I was at rock bottom, or at least what I considered being my rock bottom. My son made me brave. Brave is not a word I would have used to describe myself when I was younger but after I had my son, I found my strength. Looking at him, I found the courage to walk away from an abusive relationship. In his eyes, I saw myself as a warrior who was, and is, capable of anything. I didn't want him to be raised in a dysfunctional environment or exposed to toxic masculinity. I had to be brave so I could give my son something more. I had to figure my next steps and the path I needed to take. I enrolled in school and at one point, was juggling three jobs to make ends meet. Until finally, I was promoted to a full-time salaried position. Once I received that promotion, our lives started to feel a little better each day.

As much as my son helped me move forward, my daughter catapulted me onward even more. Eight years after the birth of my son, somehow I managed to clone myself and give birth to my mini me. Since I gave birth to my daughter, I have had a fire burning within my bones to do whatever it takes to provide her with the support she needs in every way. I want her to see that she can have anything her heart desires. She can be a powerful leader with a successful career, and have a family that adores her. In those short eight years, I had changed a lot. I had a great job, was financially stable, and I had even been able to travel on a regular basis. I knew when I got pregnant, my life would have to slow down, and I was ready to make that adjustment. After I had Taylor, I struggled with depression. I love my daughter and I have loved her since the moment I heard her heartbeat. My depression did not cause me to love her any less; she was my baby doll. After having her, my hormones were out of balance which triggered postpartum depression. The depression continued to develop when I went back to work; I couldn't find my balance. There was never enough time. When I was home, I felt guilty because my job needed me; when I was at work, I felt guilty because my children needed me. I didn't have anything left to give.

After I had my daughter, I knew I had to change. It was time for the healing work I had been trying to avoid. I knew I had a lot of learning I needed to do but I was scared. I was scared to face my fears, and I was afraid to slow down and really look at my heart. When Taylor was one, I was going through a lot of emotional turmoil. My relationship with her father had fallen apart, and I felt like I was carrying the weight of the world on my shoulders. Women are expected to carry babies, give birth, care for newborns and meet all their needs, while their bodies are trying to heal from the trauma that childbirth brings with it. I had no idea what it was like for people struggling with postpartum depression. It was intense. As hard as it was for me to feel depressed, it was even harder to admit I needed help. There is so much shame attached to postpartum depression. It is very real. Mental health is very real. If there is a time, I mean anytime you feel you need assistance, please don't feel ashamed to do so. Your well-being is the most important thing.

I had suffered so many traumas mentally and emotionally; I decided it was time to break the cycle I was in and heal, really heal. I wish I could say I did the work for myself but my children were my primary motivation. I still hadn't come to the place where I understood my own worth. I just wanted to break every generational cycle and stop any of my shortcomings and toxic behaviors from being passed to them. I knew I was carrying heavy baggage; I knew it was weighing me down. I didn't know it was also holding me back. I could feel that I was ready to move forward but couldn't seem to take the steps needed. Every time I would make a little bit of progress, something would happen and I would feel like I was being thrown in a sling-shot back to the starting blocks. I had to put down each piece of luggage and go through the contents. I knew I would have to let go of some things, find a new home for others, and repair some that have been tattered. I was scared, but I wanted to give my children the best version of myself so they could be empowered to love the best version of their selves. One by one, I opened each piece of luggage. I stared at the contents, examining each piece. I made the hard choices to repair what needed repaired, clean up what needed cleaned, let go of the things that no longer fit the woman I wanted to be, and I put away the things worth keeping. It wasn't easy. It wasn't comfortable. Growth isn't a comfortable process. It would have been easier for me to keep lugging around my baggage and staying with what was familiar, but I knew the life I wanted to give my children couldn't coexist with all this baggage; there simply wasn't enough space for them both. Children might listen to some of what you say but you better believe they listen and learn from what you do. My children watched me take a long, hard look at myself and work through my junk. Now I teach them the tools they need to sit with their pain, feel their feelings, let go of hurt, and love themselves. I model and teach a growth mindset.

At one point I would have described myself as weak, a victim even, fully believing that life was happening to me. Now I know I am a force to be reckoned with. I am an overcomer; I am strong, fearless, and I fully know my value and worth. Once I unpacked my bags, I was able to tap into all this creative energy I didn't know I had. I developed Maximum Evolution and began to build my brand. I found that flow state and things started pouring out of me. My children have watched me smash all my goals and become a confident and successful entrepreneur. They know life is not about perfection. Disappointments will happen but circumstances will not detour us from moving forward, all of us. I provide them with knowledge and direction. They know how to barter. They just don't get what they want handed to them, they make a case for whatever they want and offer something in return for that item. We have a deal; their needs, both physical and emotional, are all met and when they want something, they are prepared to work for it. I want them to understand money and how to have a good work ethic. Last year, I was able to bring them into the Maximum Evolution family and two new entrepreneurs were born. Through our collaborations, we have built two more brands; Jalen's World and Taylor's Playhouse. They have been able to help with the entire creative process of brand creation and product development. I have learned so much from them; they are intelligent, adventurous, creative, and brave.

There are some mothers that aren't the greatest and may have had their own traumatic experiences that stunted their ability to nurture. Unfortunately, we don't have the power to choose our parents. But we all have the power to decide who we want to be in this world. Your past doesn't have to define you. I can't imagine how it feels to have a bad mother or father. I can't imagine the rejection, the pain a child, young adult, even a full grown adult feels. Rejection by a parent is hurtful and can taint the soul of a child or adult. It's devastating. Motherly love is the first form of love a child experiences. It molds how they feel about themselves, how they interpret love, what love is supposed to look like, and even how it is received. We look up to our parents as super heroes, role models, but especially for love, support, guidance, empathy. It can impact the person you are even today. I have learned whether it's your mother, father, brother, sister, cousin, you must accept them for who they are and who they aren't, in order for you to truly move forward and have control over your mind, heart, body, soul. You have to let go of the mother you are yearning for and understand the person doesn't have the capacity to be what or who you need them to be. You have to forgive them. It may have been learned, it may be their own pain or the trauma experienced, the healing they needed, it may be how tainted they were as a child, and you may trigger them. There are so many factors as to why a person is the way they are. Seek healing and understanding, for yourself; there are so many resources out there to help. The goal is to heal and break the cycle for your children, to be at peace and free of any weight, pain, or trauma you are carrying, solely for you and your peace. You can't control what has happened to you but you can unlock a whole new world of opportunity by forgiving, releasing, accepting, letting go of all you have been through and moving forward.

To My Children;

Mommy loves you with all of her heart and has done the best she could from the moment you were conceived. There have been times when I have cried because I want to provide you with so much more. There are times I live in fear for you because of the things I cannot protect you from in this cold and heartless world. There are times I feel saddened by the decisions I have made because of the way it may impact your lives.

You are the most beautiful and intelligent children in this world. I am so blessed and grateful to be your mom. I will always be here to love and protect you. I will be your shoulder to cry on, and your motivator to push you forward. I am your biggest cheerleader! There are things in your life I wish I had the power to change, parts I wish I could erase so you never have to feel any pain. I hate to see anything make you sad. My only goal in life is to make you proud and for you to both know you are loved, you are enough, you are powerful, and that you have a family that loves and supports you. You have a mother that will do and sacrifice anything for you. I will do everything in my power to build a legacy for myself and the both of you so strong your children's children will never have to understand what it means to struggle. I want you both to have opportunities; the world is your oyster.

I will continue to make sure we cherish the times we have together and keep planning new and profound experiences. Your happiness and the smiles on your faces are repayment enough. You are shining bright stars and will be an unstoppable force in this world. I love you and I am here for you until my last breath.

Love,

Mommy

10

The Blame Game

"Forgiveness is the key that unlocks the door of resentment and the handcuffs of hatred. It is a power that breaks the chains of bitterness and the shackles of selfishness."

-Corrie Ten Boom

I am not perfect, far from it really. I understand now, the idea of perfection doesn't exist, despite my years of chasing it. A major shift occurred when I realized my part in the dysfunction of my life. I learned, in order to evolve, I had to take responsibility for my decisions, all of them. I had to own my mistakes and even when it was hard to see, I had to identify my role in the situation.

Like everyone, I could easily pinpoint the fault of others. I could name twenty things every person did that shaped my life negatively. I could see those lessons so clearly. I had to dig a little deeper to understand my part and the importance of taking responsibility for my actions. The blame game is destructive and feels so very justified. Especially when the other party fails to acknowledge the way they hurt you, or take responsibility for their part in any way. When someone fails to apologize, we feel owed, and we hold on to that feeling until it turns into resentment, slowly eating away at us from the inside out.

For years, I was a walking time bomb ready to explode and claim the life of everyone in my path. I didn't trust anyone. I was walled off, hiding deep within the tower I built to keep myself safe. I became enraged. I wasn't in control of my emotions; at any given moment, I could snap and lost it even because of the smallest infraction, you know, like blinking too loud or looking in the wrong direction.

The rage stemmed from unexpressed grief. Grief I had worked hard at burying, thinking it might go away on its own. I was grieving the life I imagined I would have; grieving from the way I felt inside; grieving for the little girl who had to grow up fast; grieving because of the hurt and pain others had put me through; grieving from the trauma I had experienced and the person it turned me into; grieving from the poor choices I made and the consequences I had to face; grieving all the ways I had let myself down; I was grieving from all my heart-breaks. I had so much unexpressed grief pressed as far down as it would go- then all of a sudden, I ran out of room. It all had to come out.

It wasn't until I knew I no longer wanted to suffer, and that I wanted to be free from all this grief that I realized I was actually grieving. I was carrying the weight of all this sadness, misery, anguish, and pain. It was so heavy I could barely move. I had suppressed my emotions so often it felt normal to feel numb or detached from my emotions. Grief impacts you in ways you don't even recognize until you are ready to face the pain.

At one of my lowest points, I was jobless with a newborn baby depending solely on me. Broken, ashamed, and humiliated, I felt hopeless. We have already established I was an overachiever; I had dreams, goals. I had a vision for my life and it did not include raising a newborn alone. I was disappointed in myself. I felt like I let my parents down; I knew I had let myself down. What little self-esteem I had was depleted. I was angry that I allowed myself to be put in this position and even more irate with the person that helped me get there. I held onto that anger; I let it fester. Overtime, the anger grew into a beast that could not be tamed. I grew bitter. I held onto my pain, clinging to the hurt like my badge of honor. I was miserable. One day, I caught a glimpse of my reflection and I didn't recognize the person staring back at me. She was weak, defeated, full of fear and animosity. I hated who I had become. I blamed everyone for turning me into this shell of a person who I had grown to despise.

I decided I had to protect myself; no one else would do it. I felt like everyone was out to get me. I disconnected from everyone. I pushed people away, and I kept them at arm's length. I didn't feel safe enough to let my walls down, let alone being able to let someone else in. I was lonely. My heart ached for connection but I couldn't do it. I was paralyzed with fear. I had been betrayed too many times; I believed, with everything in me, that this was how my life would always be.

We have all had experiences that have impacted us negatively. Some children are raised in environments no child should ever be in; others are abused physically, emotionally, and sexually. As a child, you do not have control over who your parents are or who you are exposed to. Children have very little control over their lives. Yet, your childhood plays a major role in the person you become.

When I was younger, I thought everyone's life at home was the same as mine. I took for granted that everyone had a family like mine. I learned, the hard way, that was not the case. When I was sixteen, I started hanging out in Edenwald. One night when I was hanging out, someone stole my Nextel from me- I was shocked. I had never had something stolen from me, lost maybe a hundred times but stolen, never; I didn't know people really did that to each other, especially to a teenager. I was hanging out with friends, thinking we were really cool, loving our newfound freedom. Nextel was the hottest thing out at the time, yes, I know this ages me. You had to be able to chirp or you just weren't fly. It even had the capability of having songs as a ringtone which was just making its way on the scene. I just bought a i95 and gave it to someone to add ringtones to and they gave me their phone in the meantime. We switched sim cards and it was perfect. I ended up just giving them my new phone and upgraded to the i730. I had left my phone behind by accident in the living room, to use the bathroom. When I returned, I didn't think about my phone or it being unsafe to leave it in a room for a minute. I didn't realize what happened until I started to look for my phone. Someone in the room had taken it. It's a strange feeling to be in a room filled with people and know someone had just taken something of yours. There were friends I knew and some people I had never seen before. I knew someone knew what happened to my phone. I was super upset, but I knew a phone is replaceable, I am not. I just left. After my phone was stolen, I never looked at that place or the people there the same. This event was the first time I realized maybe life isn't the same for all. Why would someone deem it necessary to steal from anyone? It made me sad; I felt sorry for the person. Sometimes people do things because they feel like they have no other options or they have become a product of their environment. It took me a long time to fully, really understand this but the theft of my phone was the first time I began to see this reality.

I am the type of person that wants success. I desire fulfillment. I am self-motivated. Whatever I set my mind to, I accomplish. I started my adult career with a popular hotel as a data entry clerk. I worked my way up through the company. I took advantage of trainings and on-the-job experience. I volunteered for more responsibilities. Eventually, I decided I wanted to become a General Manager. After a lot of hard-work and dedication, I was promoted within two short years of making that decision. When some people hear that, they assume that's what most people do in that line of work; they work, get promoted, and continually move up. That's not the reality. Most people stay in their position or make a lateral move when they get bored. Not me. I worked tirelessly to prove myself. I studied, I watched, I took everything in so I could understand the intricacies of every position. I worked over, all the time. People don't understand the hard-work and dedication that goes on behind the scenes. All they see is the trophy, the title. Some people expect the trophy or job handed to the others, or want to take yours.

As I was on my path of success, my goal was to help anyone along my journey, but you had to want it. I had to see the fire in your eyes. I know what alone feels like. I know what it's like to not know what your next step is or how you are going to make ends meet. If I can help you, I will. That's how I am wired. Let's learn and grow together; even if you surpass me, I will be waving you on from the sidelines like your personal cheerleader; flips, cartwheels, and all. I believe there is room for everyone to succeed.

    Unfortunately, many of the people I helped and thought were friends turned into enemies. The corporate world is harsh, especially for women. Instead of feeling like they had a chance to sit at the table with me, some felt the need to try to take my seat. I had several experiences with this; I'm not going to name drop, but there are individuals I provided an opportunity to, and in turn, they tried to sabotage my career with lies. There are individuals I supported, helped to navigate, step by step assistance, trained, developed, assisted in any way I could but all they did was just to fabricate, exaggerate, and tarnish my reputation. I considered these individuals crabs in the barrel. What sets you apart from the rest is understanding the scarcity and orphan mindset. In my mind, there is room for all of us. I am in no competition with anyone, only with myself; my goal is to be bigger, better, stronger than I was yesterday, last week, last month, last year.

Being betrayed is a different kind of hurt. Especially when you know you were genuine and your heart was in the right place. I didn't help others because I wanted a pat on the back. When I help someone, I looked at it as a gift, not like anyone owed me. For a while, I thought that way. I felt like if I took the time to support you with either time, energy, or finances at the very least, it would earn some kind of loyalty. This kind of thinking creates an unhealthy dynamic that ruins relationships. I had to learn no one owes me anything. I made a choice to help that person; I made the choice to build that relationship with them. When you pour into people, sometimes you get taken advantage of. This happened to me repeatedly in the workplace. Eventually, true colors and intentions will be exposed but most times, it's when it is too late and you have already lost something- a friend, relationship, or part of your reputation. This kind of hurt makes you feel intense pain; the way your heart is shattered can change the way you view people. It's the most detrimental feeling that I wouldn't wish on anybody. If you don't deal with this kind of hurt, you can become defensive and coldhearted because you never want to allow yourself to experience that betrayal again.

There is a reason for every person in your life. Each one has been placed there on purpose, carrying within them a lesson for you. I had to understand the way people treated me, or mistreated me, was because I allowed it. I didn't value myself enough to set boundaries and standards. I taught all of these people how to treat me by accepting the foolishness they offered. Because I made myself available, they took from me and when they did, I didn't say anything or stand up for myself; I just took it.

I had to take ownership of my life. I couldn't keep blaming everyone for the hurt I kept experiencing. I realized I no longer wanted to live in this black hole that was draining all of my life energy. I was giving away my power to the people who had hurt me. I was clinging to the anger, the hurt, and the pain. I wanted to be free of the hatred. I had to take responsibility for my part. I had to forgive myself and I had to forgive the people that hurt me. I learned to forgive quickly. Well, depending on how bad you hurt me. I could forgive someone in a minute or it may take me a couple of months but believe me, I am forgiving you. I will not carry your baggage. I am not JetBlue. I will not allow your poison to contaminate my mind, my heart, and my soul.

Accept the "I'm sorry" you will never hear or see. I have forgiven so many that have broken my heart without ever acknowledging any of it. I learned forgiveness is not about the other person. It was for me. It was for my freedom. The hurt and anger I was holding onto took a toll on me. I had become snappy for no reason. I was mean. I was emotionally hysterical raging one moment, then sobbing uncontrollably the next. I was so broken inside from all the pain I suppressed, all the anger I held in, and all the times I felt unsafe and unprotected. Every time someone hurt me, it was like they took a piece of me and I had nothing left. People often blame others for the way their lives have turned out. In life, there are so many things that are uncontrollable; the family you were born into; the environment you grew up in; the lack of support and encouragement you received; the betrayals and disappointments along the way; life circumstances. You could spend an entire lifetime blaming your past, blaming others for who you are or how you are. Life is hard. There are going to be challenges, many challenges. For a long time, I allowed my past experiences have control of my present and future. I allowed those who broke my heart, harmed me, and disappointed me and gave them space to live in my mind and the power to harden my heart. I blamed them and victimized myself for the things I went through. Please do not get me wrong; I was the victim in some circumstances. I have survived every kind of abuse you can imagine. But I could not be free and still identify as a victim. I allowed the pain to become venom running through my veins and body. I had to accept an apology I knew I was never going to receive and what was even harder, I had to forgive myself for every time I fell short.

Forgiving a person doesn't mean that you have to have them in your life. There are a number of people I have forgiven that I still don't speak to. I am a person who sees and believes in the good in everyone. I understand how a person may feel or how their past experiences might influence their actions. I have four file cabinets that you could be placed in based on your actions or lack thereof. If I love you and feel like your heart is genuine and supportive, you will go into the "I love you forever" file cabinet. My mother, father, and two children have a permanent place there. If I like you and we have connected in some way, you might find yourself in the "I rock with you" cabinet. If you have wronged me a few times but are trying to be better so you can learn and grow, you will probably go into the "IDK, Questionable" cabinet with a possibility of an upgrade when your actions reflect growth and change. If you are a full-blown demon and the things you have done should be unforgivable, trust me, while I have forgiven, even if it has taken a number of months, years, or decades, you are in the "Banished, IDC, Never AGAIN" cabinet. There is no coming back for you. I have accepted the person you are. While I still wish you the best and all the success alllllll the way over there, I have revoked your access to my life. Stay blessed, but also, stay away.

I had to forgive and let go, which isn't easy to do. For years, I felt I had to be the judge, juror, and punisher. I held onto my anger and my pain as though it was a source of comfort to my soul, and the persecution of those who had hurt me depended on me holding on to all that rage. I had to learn that holding onto the anger made the pain become toxic for my body. When you hold onto anger and resentment, it's like you are drinking poison, hoping the other person suffers. My peace, my freedom, my happiness had to become top priority. I will no longer allow anyone to rob me of it.

People are going to come into your life; some will uplift, support, and love you; others will bring chaos, dysfunction, and hurt. It's okay to feel sad, shed some tears, feel the pain, but you can't live in it. You can't hold on to the hurt and live in peace at the same time. Forgive them, forgive yourself; release them, release yourself; let it go, and move on.

11
Chameleons

Insight into character comes from listening intently to the spoken word. The physical person, their charisma, charm and dramatic flair is more often used to persuade audiences, as they use these stealth tools of disguise and deception.

-Maximilian Degenerez

People disguise themselves, hiding behind a facade created to hide their true selves from the world. Sometimes this is a conscious effort; most of the time, it's more complicated and less deliberate. People want to show the world the best parts of themselves while working hard to hide their darkness. Behind my smile was a fearful little girl, desperately wanting to be protected and taken care of. However, I wore the disguise of an independent, strong woman so well that no one knew my real needs, which left them unmet.

In the wild, chameleons manipulate their physical appearance and behavior, disguising themselves from their prey. People do this as well. I can appear to be in control and calm even when I am about ready to lose it; sometimes my face gives me away but most of the time, you would never know from the outside when I am freaking out on the inside. This is a defense mechanism and a form of self-protection. I built a protective shell that knew how to show up in order to fit in, hiding underneath, my disguise of strength.

I smiled. I smiled when I felt like crying. I smiled when I felt like screaming. I smiled when I felt like I was dying on the inside. When I was spiraling and my life seemed to be falling apart, I would reach within and pull out the strength from somewhere deep within and smile, hiding my hurt and pain. My amazing parents and family have always supported me. I just didn't realize that I was so good at disguising myself no one knew I needed help. All they saw was their daughter being strong, ambitious, and successful. They have always rooted for me and believed in me; I just didn't let them in to see the ways I needed help.

There is a dangerous kind of chameleon you need to be aware of: A chameleon able to morph into whatever you need them to be so you feel safe. This kind of chameleon camouflages their true nature, waiting patiently for you to put your guard down, to trust them, to let them in. Demons in disguise. They are able to put on a spectacular show, helping you feel safe and comfortable. These people are predators and want to take advantage of you. They need to use people up physically, emotionally, and financially. They are takers; it's all they know.

12
M.E. on Zero

"People cry, not because they're weak. It's because they've been strong for too long"
                              -Johnny Depp

I push.

I sprint forward.

I keep moving.

I know how to bury my head in the sand, totally ignoring everything, and drive forward at all costs. I have pressed on with no regard to my physical or mental health and wellbeing. I have ran entire marathons on empty, busting through every limit.

I thought this is what you had to do to be successful. Just keep going- no matter what. I strived. I demanded more from myself than was physically possible. I pushed so hard I found myself down a dark path where no light could be found. Fully enveloped in the darkness, I considered it might be easier to end it all and free myself from the constant turmoil. My soul was restless. I was exhausted. I could sleep for days and wake up tired. I was depleted; completely void of hope. It seemed like I was endlessly spinning out of control; in dire need of a break from the never-ending cycle I created.

I was sick.

I suffered from a sickness our culture encourages- demands even.

Perfectionism.

Perfectionism is a disease that devours its victims one piece at a time, leaving them depleted emotionally, physically, and spiritually. Perfectionism is the idea or illusion that you NEED to be perfect in order to receive love, acceptance, accolades, recognition... I thought I needed to be perfect in order to be loved, enough, seen, heard, successful: You name it; I believed it.

As a child, I strived to be the best. I longed to prove my worth. I needed to be better. An A wasn't enough if there was the chance to get an A+. "Good job" wasn't enough when "Great job" was available. If I had just enough, I wanted more. I created a cycle of longing, wanting, and striving. I was trying to obtain my worth through perfection. I was playing a game I could never win.

I cannot remember a time in my life when I didn't demand perfection from myself. I would often create a tornado of chaos surrounding the effort needed to achieve the impossible feat I thought would help me feel enough; smart enough; successful enough; beautiful enough; worthy enough. Fighting the pull of the tornado drained everything I had. The constant chaos felt normal because it was all I ever knew. Exhaustion felt like my normal state of being, even as a child. I couldn't stop because I had to prove myself. If I slowed down, what if someone else passed me by? What if someone else got a better grade? Made more friends? Got the boy? Got the degree? Got the promotion? Got the husband? Figured out parenting?

I spent every day searching for peace. I thought it was something external I had to find or achieve. I was mad that no one could give me the steps to peace. Where was the "to do" list? I wanted the specifics- do these things and you will be successful and feel at peace. I wanted to be able to check off each step and receive my gold star. There was no list. Well, there is a lot of lists people will sell you on how to achieve peace- and I tried most of them but surprisingly, they never worked.

I wanted to be free of these mental and emotional chains I couldn't seem to break. Finally, I got fed up with the way I felt. I started to look back on my life and try to figure out where all this began. I didn't really know what I was looking for but I knew my need for perfectionism came from needing to feel like I was in control. I needed to feel like I was the one in control of everything. So I looked back and examined my life to identify the first time I felt out of control, helpless, and terrified.

Then a memory popped into my mind; I think I was around 5 or 6 years old. I was sitting on my bunk bed watching chaos ensue. I remember feeling scared and completely powerless. Dysfunction felt normal because it was what I was used to living in, but this was different. I often felt powerless, completely out of control, and full of fear as a child. I wanted to do something, anything, to make it stop. I was always paralyzed, frozen in fear, screaming on the inside, yet unable to make an actual sound come out of my mouth. This is where it began. I had found the root of my fear and need to control everything.

Perfectionism has been a constant battle for me. I want everything to be perfect. If life has taught me anything, it is that nothing is ever perfect. Perfectionism is a form of control. I have experienced so many things that left me feeling powerless, weak, and out of control that I latched on to anything that was even seemingly controllable. I can make anything perfect in my mind; a design, a project, a styled look, my appearance. My desire for perfection has left me paralyzed. Trying to be perfect has held me back from truly showing up how I want to and kept me from attending that event, posting content, or releasing a project because of my need for things to be perfect before I can do anything. I had to learn to let go. I had to learn to release fear and control. No matter what I do, someone will have something to say. No matter how well thought out a plan is, something unexpected can happen. I have had to learn that worrying will get me nowhere but wrapped in a big ball of stress. I can do the best I can and that's it. I can only control my actions. I had to let go of the people-pleasing and the fear of man. I had to let go of the caring about other's opinions. One saying I love is, "A Lion doesn't care about what the sheep thinks." Most negative opinions are coming from those who are doing worse than you or suffer with their own insecurities. I will only accept constructive criticism from those who want me to truly succeed and are on a higher level than me. It took me a number of years to know and understand the ways of the world and the functions of other people. It is a challenge to change your thought process and mindset especially when it is all you have known and been accustomed to. I came to a realization and acceptance that there are mindsets I need to remove and transform, and perfectionism was one of them. It can literally consume your life and hold you back. I have places to go, things to achieve, and a world to conquer.

    I love to help people. Looking back, it seems as if my entire life was spent trying to save everyone around me; sometimes (a lot of times if I am honest) at the expense of my own wellbeing. After working through my own healing, I realized I was trying to be for everyone else what I needed. I exhausted myself trying to care for, protect, rescue, and love others because I needed someone to do the same for me. I felt unworthy of love. I felt like there was a reason I was not enough. I felt like there was a defect in myself that caused bad things to happen to me and the people around me. All of these feelings led to a lifetime of striving and trying to validate myself.

    I strived to be the best; the head cheerleader; the top of the class; the employee of the month; the employee of the year; promotion after promotion. I never celebrated an achievement; they were never enough. Every time I accomplished something, I looked to the next thing and started the entire process over. I have so many certifications; pieces of paper to tell you I am qualified. I have received so many promotions as I worked my way up the corporate ladder from an entry level position all the way to the GM. I accomplished every goal I had and guess what? I never felt satisfied.

    Years of striving left me drained. I had nothing left to give. I began to resent the people I helped through the years; why was no one there for me? I had given so much of myself away to everyone else and nothing was left. My cup wasn't just empty- it had been shattered into a million pieces. Why wasn't anyone there to help me pick up the pieces? I got angry, then I got sad, then angry again, but mostly tired. I was tired of the striving and feeling less than. I was tired of trying to prove my worth. I was tired of trying to achieve the next thing. I was tired of living the facade I created. I was done.

My body was screaming for me to rest, to step back, and give myself time to heal. I was experiencing constant headaches, which turned into migraines. My immune system was compromised; I started getting sick all the time. I was in a depressive state; all I wanted to do was sleep. I was trying to run a marathon on zero.

Your mental and emotional state will dictate your every move, even without you knowing it. Some people are more optimistic and can more easily align to a sense of peace and contentment. I am not that person. It takes work for me; a lot of work. I think some people are born more optimistic; I also think our childhood and traumas play a huge role in our ability to align with peace. I think my case is a combination of being born with a personality that is more driven and a little skeptical, and when paired with childhood trauma, peace and contentment, it seemed almost unattainable.

Since I had the revelation of when the perfectionism started and when the need to control things started, I have been able to do a deep work on myself. I have changed. I understand I don't have control over anything in my life, only the way I respond to it. I have learned how to identify the way perfectionism shows up in my life (although I am trying to do so faster). I see how I have used self-sabotage in the past out of fear in my career and relationships. I have learned how to work through those feelings as they arise. I know when I start to try to numb myself so I don't have to feel. I have learned how to take care of my health and my emotional wellbeing. When I get stuck, I work with a wellness and/or business coach in order to identify obstacles so I know how to move forward. I am learning how to relax.

It's not an easy journey. It's hard to break habits and learned behaviors that are rooted deep within your soul. I made the choice. The powerful choice, that I wanted something different for my life. I wanted and needed a really drastic change and not just for me, but also for my children. They needed me, but they needed me to be present and not just there with the capacity to nurture them. When I was running on zero, they paid the price. Sometimes my physical body was there but my mind was still at work. I want them to know how to care for themselves physically, emotionally, and professionally, but how could I teach them something I didn't know? They might have been my motivation for taking the time to heal myself but in the end, I am glad I did it for me.

I lean into my emotional turmoil now, so I can learn from it. I know the lesson hold within it, the healing I need. I believe there is greatness on the inside of everyone, even me. I am more than a certificate, degree, promotion, or any material wealth I can imagine. I understand that achieving goals and accolades will not make me feel whole or satisfied. I know I cannot fill any voids with temporary happiness. I have learned how to show up for myself; how to love myself.

13

Deception

"Trust is like a mirror; you can fix it if it's broken, but you can still see the crack in the reflection."

-Lady Gaga

Deception is the deliberate intent to fabricate, manipulate or conceal to mislead intentionally. The act of being deceived, even in the smallest of ways, is cruel and can feel as if you are being shattered in a million pieces. Sometimes deception causes you to feel as though the world, as you know it, is going to end. There are some evil people in this world and potentially, some of those evil people have made their way into your circle. Once you have been deceived by someone, if you aren't careful, it will impact the way you trust every person in your life.

Who do you trust? Who can you trust? How do you trust? Especially after you feel like you have been deceived. Who is in your corner? Who has your back? Who truly loves you? Who really wants the best for you? These are the questions that keep you up at night after you have been deceived.

Sometimes deception becomes a part of a person to the point that they no longer are able to recognize the deception, dishonesty, or deception in their behaviors. There are those who view deceiving others as a sport of which they are masters. They are on a relentless pursuit of what they want and have no regard for those who they hurt in the process. Deception is a form of manipulation; it's a way to gain power. People that use deception as a way to control others are unable to care about the people in their lives; they see people as a means to an end. The only thing that matters is what you can do for them. All situations and relationships are about them; they generally don't care about what others think or feel, although this reality is well masked.

People that deceive are great pretenders with deep-rooted issues. It takes a specific makeup for someone to be able to consistently lie or pretend to be someone they aren't. Master manipulators are so skilled at deception that their victims are often confused, second guessing everything, and trying to blame themselves for whatever mess just occurred. If you have dealt with many people like this, it's likely to distort your perception of the entire human race. You will begin to question everything you think you know about your relationship with a manipulator. Why do they feel the need to lie? Why do they feel the need to hide things? Were any of their feelings real? Did they ever really love me? What did I do to make them cheat on me? These questions are just the tip of the iceberg. Once you have encountered a deceptive person, you will pick yourself trying to understand what happened.

There are some very deceptive men and woman who seem attractive, smart, strong, and confident. They are natural performers with the ability to bend the truth. It can be truly difficult to pinpoint their deceptive behaviors until you are already entangled with them in ways that seem too difficult to break free from. Looking back, you will probably notice red flags; we sometimes miss or even choose to ignore our gut checks, red flags, and our intuition. After years of being victim of master manipulators and full time deceivers, I have learned this and how to discern deceptive people quickly. They always give themselves away; it's up to you to be honest in evaluating the situation, listen to your gut, and recognize master manipulators before they wreak havoc in your life!

There have been a number of times I have been deceived and played for a fool. What is the saying, "Fool me once, shame on you…Fool me twice… shame on me…. fool me for the thousandth time….now I'm just your fool" or however the saying goes. I have been deceived so many times it began to feel familiar; I had become the fool. Although it would make life so much easier if there was a sign or stamp on each person's forehead telling you exactly who they are; at one time, I would have still wanted to learn for myself. I think if the person could have a stamp that reads R U N...T U R N A R O U N D... or RUN FOR THE HILLS... I would be like hmmmm...I wonder why. Let's go find out.

Deception undermines trust.

Trust.

Trust is a small word to describe such a big feeling. When trust is broken, it shatters, making it almost impossible to put the pieces back together. I have struggled with trust; understanding it, maintaining it, and believing it is even possible.

Trusting people has not come naturally to me. I poured time, energy, and even finances into people who did nothing but take from me. After being taken advantage of time after time, I began to build a protective wall around my heart. By the time I realized the wall existed, it was an impenetrable fortress. No one could enter because the walls were too high to climb; I was trapped in a prison. My heartbreak and disappointment became my jailer.

This wall created an abrasive attitude I used as a defense mechanism. My shield of protection kept people that would have been good for me away. Sometimes I would be controlling, other times I could be completely indifferent. My attitude. Don't get me started. A.T.T.I.T.U.D.E. I had it. My communication style was all over the place; over communicating to the point of annoyance or avoiding conversations all together. I think I might have been the reason for the invention of the term 'ghosting'. It has taken me a long time to understand the reason behind all these behaviors. I acted out because of hurt, hurt I tried to bury, run from, deny, control, and excuse anything but deal with. All of the times my trust was broken, it created a deep, dark root within me that seemed unable to remove.

    I see the best in people. It's one of my gifts; however, it has also been my biggest obstacle. After spending a short time with someone, I see their purpose, the best version of themselves. Where I error is that sometimes I can see the potential and choose to focus on that, ignoring every red flag, every voice of caution. I decided who this person could be and set my mind to that instead of seeing the person standing before me. Sometimes people aren't ready to be the best version of themselves. More times than I can count, I have wanted something for someone more than they wanted for themselves. I pushed, I invested time, money, and so much energy trying to help them that I never stopped to think maybe they weren't ready, or maybe they were using me. They say once a person shows you who they are the first time- believe them. Even after all I have been through, I still have difficulty with this.

My heart is pure and kind. I want what is best for people. I want the best for people. I believe that people are the same and can't imagine they could ever do things that would hurt me because I am using the way I treat others as my measuring stick. I can't even count on two hands the number of times that I have been stabbed in the back. It is the most frustrating thing because I wasn't able to understand why I kept allowing myself to be surrounded by these sophisticated snakes. What is about me that attracts them? What is it about me that I continually seem to be connected to them? Why do I keep ending up in the bed, under a blanket, crying because of how someone hurt me in the most detrimental way? Why do I keep giving power and fuel to these people? Why am I so trusting? I beat myself up every time after the catastrophic unveiling of the person's true self and intent. As if it is my fault, why didn't I pay attention to the signs? Why did I ignore every time I was shown? So many questions I asked myself as I sat with my tears. My pain. My heartbreak. How did I end up here, AGAIN? For the millionth time.

When someone hurts me, I assume it was a huge mistake and give them another chance; then another; then another. Finally, after riding the cycle out over twenty times, I snap. I see it. I believe it. Up rises the protective shield; snap, you are ghosted. Blocked forever. I can be standing in the same room and you are Casper, the non-friendly ghost, to me.

Now, when I am hurt, there are two options; either wrath and rage or saying nothing at all. I choose the latter until I have processed what and how I feel. The goal is to no longer react but only respond. No one has power over me, unless I give it to them. Which I try never to do. I have moments where I may regress but I forgive myself quickly and move forward, remembering I am no one's victim. The hurt and pain inflicted by the person is a direct reflection of them, not me. Unfortunately, we all have to trust people to a certain extent; we all need people in our circle. While that is true, you get to determine the capacity in which you want them in that circle. Not everyone is meant for your circle. It is not mandatory for your family members to be in your circle. Toxic and deceptive is toxic and deceptive no matter what title the person holds. The deception I experienced altered my mental and emotional processes forever. Those that were sent to be guardians, to fill me with love and support were pushed away; I kept them out. I felt it was too good to be true. I have missed out on many healthy and genuine people due to my own blinders.

When I was younger, there was a person near and dear to me but because of all the let downs, I sabotaged it. The broken trust, combined with the impenetrable wall and all the defense mechanisms, caused a feeling of unworthiness that would not permit a healthy relationship. When you are younger, you don't necessarily realize how your life has been impacted or tainted. You are still learning and figuring out who you are as an individual. You are very impressionable. I never realized how deep my trust and love was so tainted. It literally was the determining factor of how I navigated through life. I have a more clear perception of cause and effect, referring to how people navigate through life.

I had a best friend in middle school I did everything with. We were tight, spending as much time as we could together outside of school, sleepovers, and hanging out. One day, she up and moved; it broke my heart. Other people I considered friends stole from me, lied to me, let me down, and gossiped about me. Family members betrayed me, lied about me and caused me so much unnecessary drama, as well as mistreating me. I never allowed myself to get attached and for so long. I regret the way I behaved and wished I could take it back. There was nothing I could do to change it. I beat myself up about it for so long. They were the first to truly care and show up for me. I ruined it because I was tainted by all the deception I have experienced. I had to forgive myself and let go of the regret. How could I do better if I don't know better? I have been solely focused on healing my heart and learning new ways to discern and analyze my behaviors, as well as my decision with the people I've met and have in my life. I have to quickly make the decision of who this person is and what purpose they are serving to my journey. Are they here as a distraction or truly meant to be on this journey called life?

14

Nemesis

When you do well, everybody's after you, and sometimes the motives are legitimate, and sometimes it's envy and jealousy.
-Robert Kraft

There is a difference between being triggered because one has something you desire which causes jealousy versus acting on the jealousy. What do I mean? There are times you may see someone in the car you want to own, the nice house, the beautiful partner, nice clothes, the body. It may conjure up some feeling because you want it too. You want the money, the home, the clothes, the great personality, the popularity etc. You work towards making it happen for yourself. You celebrate and are excited for the success of the person. You are happy for the person who was able to make those things happen for yourself. You know your time will come and it is only used as motivation to work just a little harder to make the things your heart desires most come into fruition. Now, there are those who act on those jealous emotions. They will do things subconsciously and consciously to sabotage the individual with those things. They do underhanded and low-key things to hurt the individual. They try to get others to dislike you by making jokes with underlying insults, or bad-mouth your character. Mainly due to the lack they feel within themselves; the crab in the barrel and scarcity mindset.

Then there are those who are envious; this is a whole different type of person. They feel they deserve what you have and are on a mission to take it away from you by any means necessary. Jealousy is a disease, but envy is deadly.

The challenge with all of this is that most of the time, it is the people that are closest to you, which is the worst part. Sometimes you are unable to know the difference or who these individuals are. Through time, the truth will always come to light; hopefully you will see the truth before it's too late.

Those who are jealous or envious can't comprehend behind the scenes work it takes, the sacrifices you've made, and dedication it takes to have the things you have. They see the tip of the tree blooming and flourishing, but have no idea of the complicated root system the tree has to have to survive. They see your success; high paying job, nice bags and clothes, your home, the cars, and the wealth but they missed the year it took and the blood sweat and tears you put into everything you have. They don't understand all you had to do to accomplish your goals and to be where you are today. When people treat you like this, it can be so disappointing. It breaks my heart when I see genuine, loving, empathetic, supportive people hurt because of someone else's jealously or envy.

Some people naturally have a jealous mindset. They have learned to be jealous and often feel like they are owed everything. This can be genetic or environmental but usually, it's a combination of both. This is why it's so important for us to understand the patterns we learn from our families and how to break them.

Sometimes jealously forms because people are a part of groups that have never had enough and had to fight each other for resources. You wouldn't be jealous or envious if you understood there is room for everybody to eat. This is a systematic problem that needs to be addressed at a national level so that every child can have a quality education, access to health care, and opportunities for a future.

If you begin to feel jealousy trying to manifest, make the powerful choice; instead of becoming a green-eyed monster, find out how those individuals made things happen for themselves, learn from them, and allow hope for your life to grow. What do you need to do or learn so you can begin on your own path? Look at people succeeding as inspiration!

The trait to hate is not in my DNA at all. If I see someone that has something I want, it might trigger me, but I will never hate or allow my negative feelings to turn into resentment. I know that these feelings are solely about me and has nothing to do with the person. I work hard to understand why I feel the way I do. I choose to celebrate and congratulate others of their successes. The difference is I know all will fall into place in due time. I no longer have a scarcity mindset. I believe there is enough space for everyone to have success and enough space for everyone to have a seat at the table. I do not need to dim anyone else's light or pull the seat from under anyone. For a very long time, I was resentful and didn't understand why people treated me the way they did. Why did people intentionally leave me out? Why did this person embarrass me in front of others? Why did this person try to sabotage my career? Why didn't this person celebrate my successes the way I celebrated theirs? Why didn't this person support me the way I supported them? Why did this person do a complete 180 once I got my promotion? Why was this person so mean and disrespectful? Why did this person steal from me? Why did this person make fun of the way I look? Why does this person treat me so poorly? Why did this person betray me? There were so many questions, each of which had real hurts attached to them.

    I have always lived my life trying to be kind and always helping others. If I were to write down the amount of times I have helped someone, even when I didn't even have the energy to help myself, I would have a scroll from here to Egypt. I never did anything for a pat on the back or for a trophy. I only did it because I knew what it felt like to feel alone or have no clue how I was going to make things happen. It gives me nothing but satisfaction to know that I helped someone even in a small way.

When I grew in the corporate world, I wasn't excited about the power. I was excited to have the ability to give opportunities that would change lives. I had the opportunity to provide a seat at the table, let alone a space to stand in the room. My goal in life is to have the financial capacity to change lives, provide opportunities, and to help others achieve their goals and dreams. I am not an individual who has to be the only shining star in the room. I want to help light other stars and bring others with me on the journey. There are those who do not like that and hated how others loved me. They hate how I am intelligent and kind. I am nowhere near perfect; I have my ways and can be mean if I am rubbed the wrong way. I am very big on energy and vibes. If it feels off, then I will always listen to my intuition. There have been many times that I didn't and it led me to the path of betrayal, back-stabbing, and sheer disappointment.

For many years, I dimmed my light to allow others to feel better about themselves or dumbed myself down so I wouldn't be the smart know-it-all. I would be extra mindful of the way I dressed to make sure I didn't outshine anyone. I did so many things to accommodate everyone else's feelings but my own. When it came time for my feelings to be at the forefront, most of the time, no one cared.

I have so many experiences I could share, most of which would shock you. Jealousy and envy played a major part. I used to beat myself up about it all, until I realized the issue was something I couldn't control. The only thing I could control was my reaction or removing myself from the situation.

The main reason I am not a jealous or envious person is because I learned to stop comparing myself to anyone else. I am only in competition with myself. I am content with who I am and if there is anything I want to change, I take ownership on myself to work and change myself. I don't spew any of my fears or any insecurity on anyone else. I like to put myself in rooms with individuals that are ahead of the game and are in better positions than me so I can learn and grow. I don't need to diminish someone else to make myself feel better. Most of my characteristics have been instilled in me and some was learned through experiences and growth.

> *"Comparison is and will always be the thief of joy."*
> *-Lisa Nichols*

The goal in life is to be surrounded by people who truly want to see you happy and successful. I have spent so much time being around the wrong people that I'm ready to be around selfless, independent, like-minded, confident entrepreneurs. If you have people that drain the life from you or make you feel less than, run. If you have someone who constantly gives underhanded compliments, run. If you have someone who has been exposed as a snake, run. This is the zero-tolerance era. We have all accepted and allowed the bullshit for way too long. It is time to have a tribe that wants to add value to your table. It's time to have people who are ready to help you achieve your goals and provide support. It is time to have individuals that will show up to your events and buy your merch. It is time to have people in the audience screaming and cheering when you get your awards. It is time to be surrounded by love, encouragement, and genuine support.

15

Turning your Brokenness into your Beauty

"I had to take a moment and look at my life and go, all of it, every bit has been to get you to where you are today; to get to your freedom, you had to go through those things. You had to live who you weren't to know who you are."

-Jada Pinkett Smith

As I sit completely still and listen to my heart and soul, I have come to the realization that through all of my adversities, challenges, failures, victories, wins, and happiest moments, each has played a part in shaping who I am today. Without each one of my experiences, I might still be sitting in an abusive relationship trying to survive the day. I may have just settled and worked in a little office and played it safe. All of my transgressions and experiences forced me out of my comfort zone. They pushed me past my limits.

A caterpillar goes through a long metamorphosis in order to transform into a butterfly. Just like the caterpillar, if you want to transform, you have to spend time in the cocoon. It isn't an easy process; you have to go in alone, be patient, and allow the process to take place. You will probably shed many tears, even have some emotional breakdowns, feel anxious, maybe even feel terrified. It's dark and uncomfortable. You may not know left from right or what your next step should be. Trust the process, have faith. Understand everything happens for a reason. You may not know why it is happening in the moment but there is a purpose. It is either to align you to your path or show you areas you need to learn.

Four years ago, I entered into my cocoon. I had to shed so much of my old self, letting go of the identities I created. I didn't know what was on the other side of my transformation but I knew there was more for me in this life. I had to learn to appreciate my journey. The road traveled wasn't an easy or simple one. Most see the end product and forget all the hard work that was put into becoming the person they are today. I will be frank and say for a long time, I resented my journey; all the hurt, the pain, disappointments, and failures left me angry and resentful. Negative thoughts consumed my mind and heart, robbing me of my joy, peace, leaving me unable to celebrate myself and/or my wins.

I had to learn to be present for each moment versus worrying and stressing about the things I cannot control. I had to stop allowing other people have power over my emotions. I had to take control of my thoughts and actions. I could no longer allow fear to consume and debilitate my greatness. For so long, I was consumed by my pain. One day, I was fed up and decided I was done. I wasn't going to allow those whose sole purpose was to break me down and to see me fail win; it wasn't an option.

Four years ago, I started my journey of transformation. If you think you can just blink and become a different person, let me be the first to tell you that isn't the case. I made the decision that I cannot be who I want to be in this world without some help. I needed a breakthrough, a healing journey, and I was determined to change. I found the help I needed and I haven't looked back since. There are some journeys and adversities you cannot walk alone on; you sometimes need help and the support to navigate through old hurts. Trust me, your favorite people have mentors, therapists, executive coaches, business coaches, and spiritual coaches. There are some things you just cannot learn on your own.

During times of my transformation journey, I would wake up in the middle of the night, unable to sleep. My mind would be racing; I would go through social media and watch motivational and inspirational videos, and watch them to bring some peace to the anxiety, frustration, and negative emotions I was feeling. I stumbled across a clip of Lisa Nichols' interview. I never heard of her a day in my life, but what she said in the short 30 sec clip I saw caught my interest. I had to find the whole video; I searched her name and went through all of her videos to find it. It was her interview with Tom Bilyeu. The video was FIFTY-FIVE minutes long. I instantly thought there was no way I'm watching this whole thing; forty-six minutes and thirty-seven seconds later, there I was, glued to my phone with tears streaming down my face. The video changed my life. It had to be almost three in the morning; it was so powerful. It felt as if I was meant to be up and find this video. I joined her online events, and even flew to Chicago to one of her Abundance Now events- POWERFUL. I volunteered at her Abundance Now event here in New York City; went to her Speak and Write Conference in Atlanta. The first anthology I co-authored was with the women I met at Speak and Write in Atlanta. All of these moments were life changing experiences; all it took was for me to be in radical action, remain teachable, willing to be uncomfortable, and trust the process. All I had to do was hang out in my cocoon and soak up everything I could.

One day, without warning, it was time. I emerged from my cocoon, transformed and ready to take over the world. I birthed Maximum Evolution and I have been building its foundation ever since. I created an entire beauty line, and have written or co-authored five books. I have online courses and host regular group coaching events. I have been able to share my story at many events and with individuals I work with one-on one. I am not saying any of this as a way to brag or draw attention to my accomplishments but rather, to inspire you of what is possible when you are willing to heal. If it wasn't for all that I have been through, all the doors that were opened from radical action, I wouldn't have had the confidence, the faith, and the courage to take the leap and become a full-time entrepreneur. I wouldn't be the person I am today, not even close.

Life is about being perfectly imperfect. Most of us strive for greatness; we want to be at our best and put our best foot forward, looking and feeling our best. Life has a way of moving and forcing you into the place you are meant to be by putting you in the most uncomfortable positions until you have learned the lesson or final action, or the step you needed to take. Remember the power is in our own hands ultimately; we owe it to ourselves, our children, and to the world to be the best we can possibly be. Even if you are going through a dark time, remember, it always passes. As long as you keep the faith in yourself and appreciate each new day you have been allowed to be a part of.

We get consumed and engulfed by the things we need or want, the goals we haven't achieved or what our lives are supposed to look like, or where we are supposed to be. Let all of that go and appreciate what you do have, have gratitude for those in your life supporting your dreams, wiping your tears, loving on you. Appreciate how far you have come and how much you have evolved and changed. Think about those who are in a worse position or sitting in the same space and place for the past ten years; there will always be those who have it worse. There are those who don't have the option to live another day. Stop comparing yourself to others. Your path and journey is unique to you. It doesn't matter who is ahead of you or behind you. You are only in competition with yourself. There is always going to be something more you want from life; the next goal, trip, car, house, or outfit you need to have. Enjoy the moments and things you do have with the people who truly love and support you. There will always be the more, but the time and moments that have passed, you can't ever get back.

  We all have an opportunity to continue to learn and grow, each day. If you think for one moment that you have nothing more to learn or to change, let me be the first to tell you, there is so much more for all of us to learn, no matter your age. Times are forever changing; life is continually evolving which means you can continue growing and learning mentally, emotionally, physically, socially, economically, and technologically. There will always be an opportunity for you to be better than the person you were yesterday. If you begin to feel like there is no more room for you to evolve, this is simply not the case. If you think those who you look up to don't have room to evolve and learn, you are sadly mistaken. This way of thinking will hold you back and limit your capabilities. We all have so much we can learn; most older people think it's hard to understand technology but given the right instruction, they can master even the newest gadgets. For entrepreneurs like myself, we need to remember to keep up on the newest aspects of business, marketing, and finances. We all need to continually evolve and transform.

  The beauty in all of it is to know where you are and be content with it, while at the same time knowing you have goals and dreams, and work toward them every single day. Celebrate the small wins the same way you would celebrate the biggest victories. For those who don't celebrate themselves, please, please do; celebrate yourself, be proud of your accomplishments and love yourself.

  The power is knowing who you are and all that you are capable of. You can only maintain that power if you understand how to be in charge of your emotions and stop letting your emotions be in charge of you. You have to understand your emotional health and take care of limiting mindsets so you can align with your power and build the life you want.

The beauty is to understand that you can have a relapse in your thinking for a moment, but you don't have to allow yourself to stay there. You have to learn that we all make mistakes and sometimes we will fail, but each mistake contains a powerful lesson. When we fail at something, it's not time to quit but rather to reevaluate to understand what exactly worked and what didn't, then try again. Sometimes the smallest recalibrations are the very thing that changes everything and creates the perfect climate for our wildest dreams to come true!

The beauty is being able to discern a person's intentions and heart a mile away. The beauty is being connected to your intuition and peace, and be able to navigate through any situation or challenge. The beauty is being so confident that not one soul on this planet can ruffle your feathers. The beauty is the strength in your "no' and setting healthy boundaries. The beauty is knowing your value and not settling for anything less than you deserve; knowing you add value to any table. The beauty is in loving yourself every day and every moment through self-care and self-love. The beauty is knowing perfection doesn't exist; we are all flawed. The beauty is knowing all you need to succeed is already within you. The beauty is knowing you are only in competition with yourself. The beauty is being content with who you are and understanding the person you are working to be. The beauty is being happy for others' success even if you aren't where you want to be. The beauty is not comparing yourself to others because we all have our own unique journey. The beauty is understanding that your past and present does not define your future, as long as you are in radical action. The beauty is understanding small wins and small steps towards the bigger dreams and goals. The beauty is forgiving and letting go quickly. The beauty is to know you forever need to learn and grow. The beauty is knowing being free from mental and emotional bondage. The beauty is doing it afraid, not letting fear hold you back. The beauty is taking a leap of faith on yourself. The beauty is to understand that any failure is an opportunity to assess and rise up again. The beauty is to be so comfortable in your own skin; the opinions of others won't matter. The beauty is to understand the eagle and snake, the turtle and the giraffe, the lion and the sheep. The beauty is knowing you aren't where you want to be in life but you have the power to change it. You are a warrior with the power to turn your brokenness into your beauty.

THANK YOU

FOLLOW ME

@CHANELSPENCERNOW

ACKNOWLEDGEMENTS

Adisa Thompson
Thank you for your sacrifice and dedication during the 2020 pandemic and every day. You are truly a blessing and appreciated.
candee6@gmail.com,
https://www.instagram.com/honeybee207/

Andrew Atkinson
Andrewatkinson630@gmail.com,
https://www.instagram.com/mann0676/

Rochelle, Aubrey and Madisyn Duplessis
Pretty Girl Code, Info.prettygirlcodesisters@gmail.com,
http://prettygirlcode.com/

Brittany Henry
hbbrittany24@yahoo.com,
https://www.instagram.com/__imthatgirll/

Cheryl Hayes
cheryl-marie@hotmail.com,
https://www.instagram.com/insta.cherylm/

Chris Lee
Chrisleesolo@gmail.com,
https://www.instagram.com/radiohostchris/

Christina Lopez
Modé Curves, info@modecurves.com,
http://instagram.com/modecurves

Danielle Batiste
Diabetes Made Better LLC , dmbatiste@yahoo.com, Www.daniellebatiste.com

Danielle Matthews
Be.YOU.ty Treats, noviesbeautytreats@gmail.com, http://instagram.com/be.you.ty__treats

Darling Moore
divamoore@livingwithdivatude.com, https://livingwithdivatude.com/

Deena C. Brown, PhD
Renaissance Leadership Solutions, drdeena@drdeenaspeaks.com
https://www.instagram.com/drdeenaspeaks/

Dwight Headley
Shine! headdwight2@gmail.com, https://www.instagram.com/alien_gunzalez/

Felicia Baxley
The Creative Grind, https://www.thecreativesgrind.com/

Garon Johnson
Just My Perspective Photography, justmyperspective89@gmail.com, https://www.instagram.com/justmyperspective_/

Georgia Law'rence
Georgia LAWrence LLC, Georgialaw21@gmail.com, http://www.georgialawrence.com/

Glynis Toler
bestsellingauthor@gmail.com, https://www.instagram.com/teratoler/

Heather Holland
Heather Holland Insurance,
Heatherhollandinsurance@gmail.com,
https://heatherholland.cardtapp.me/

Hopeton Barnett
Antarctica Media Group, Hbarnett05@gmail.com,
https://www.instagram.com/00grine/

Jack and Claire Hammel
Hammel Consultants, info@hammelconsultants.com,
https://www.hammelconsultants.com/

Jacquetta Coleman
Dominion Travel Services, anewthing720@gmail.com,
https://www.instagram.com/dominiontravelservices/

Jeneea J. Moore
Saved Over Success, Savedoversuccess@gmail.com,
https://www.instagram.com/savedoversuccess/

Jodi Clarke
Super proud of you and all that you have accomplished and will continue to achieve. Thank you for your sacrifice and dedication during the 2020 pandemic. You are truly an inspiration. I appreciate your support and friendship for all of these years.
lookitsjojo@gmail.com,
https://www.instagram.com/ohmyitsjojo/

John R. Solema
Solforth, john.solema@solforth.com, https://solforth.com/

Katrina Johnson

katrinajohnson000@gmail.com,
https://www.instagram.com/katrinaj7777/

Kelon Miller
Creative Elements Photography, Kelonmiller1@gmail.com,
https://www.instagram.com/kmillz101/

Kilimanjaro Toussaint
Kilimanjaro's Peak inc, Kiltoussaint83@gmail.com,
https://www.instagram.com/kilincorporated/

Latika Vines
Visionary Initiatives, LLC, info@visionary-initiatives.com,
www.visionary-initiatives.com

Lindsey Vertner
Lindsey Vertner LLC, gethappy@lindseyvertner.com,
www.lindseyvertner.com

Lovenia "COACH LOVE" Barkley
Keepsake Motivation, love@keepsakemotivation.com,
https://keepsakemotivation.com/

Marlon Knight
marlonknight80@gmail.com,
https://www.instagram.com/real_cool_boyy/

Michelle Otibo
Meesh Treats, https://www.instagram.com/meesh_treats/

Marlene Jarrett
Noli Fashion, Marlene.Jarrett@hotmail.com,
www.NoliFashion.com

Monica D. Reed

Legacy Solutions LLC,
legacybuildingconsulting@gmail.com,
https://www.instagram.com/monicadreed/

Nicholas J. Wedlow
Unfaltering Fathers LLC, nicholasjwedlow@gmail.com,
www.nicholasjwedlow.com

Nicola Harvey
ColaLovesBeauty, Colalovesbeauty@gmail.com,
www.Colalovesbeauty.com

Noreen N. Henry
Noreen N. Henry, noreennhenry@gmail.com,
www.noreennhenry.com

Sharon Nisbett
Sharon_nisbett@yahoo.com

Sheldine Victor
Sheldine Victor, sheldinev819@gmail.com,
https://www.facebook.com/sheldine.gordon

Stevii Aisha Mills
Stevii Productions, stevii@stevii.com,
www.cultivatingyouritfactor.com/

Teasha Jenea Ross
TBLV Management Group LLC,
teasha@iamteashajenea.com, www.IAmTeashaJenea.com

Thadrick Parker
Thadrick@gmail.com,
https://www.instagram.com/ttparker1976/

Theo Johnson

The Transformation, tjay0998@gmail.com, https://www.instagram.com/the_transformation88/

Therisa Means
Therisa M. LLC, ItsTherisa@TherisaM.com, https://www.therisam.com/

Vernae Taylor
Triple Threat Vision LLC , vernaet@gmail.com, https://www.instagram.com/vernaetaylor/

Yvonne Brown
Affirm & Pursue Academy, yvonnebrown09@gmail.com, https://yvonnebrown.podia.com/

Stand 4 Sisterhood, established December 21, 2016, as a 501(c)(3) not-for-profit organization by Marguritte S. Johnson, in Dallas. Marguritte serves the community as a social activist. She has an International Doctorate of Christian Counseling from Grace International Bible University.

S4S is commissioned to strategically sustain under-served and under-resourced girls and women, both personally and professionally, via mentoring, advocacy and prevention.

The purpose of S4S is to eliminate the economic, mental and social barriers for girls and women resulting in poverty, gender inequality, and relentless cycles of abuse and addiction.

Furthermore, the vision of S4S is to enrich girls and women globally with a foundation of identity that will empower them to live, lead and leave a legacy for generations to follow.

To bring sincere support, hope and sustainability to girls and women, S4S will reintegrate the power of 'Each one, Reach one' via the strategic implementation of inter-generational mentoring.

4Core: The Mentor Movement will serve as a catalyst of change to catapult our society into proactive solutions by presenting opportunities for girls and women from all generations to connect, engage, exchange and share their W.E.L.L. (**W**isdom, **E**xperiences, **L**ove and **L**egacy), while paying it forward as a collective cohort.

The supporters in our community that unashamedly **SpeakUP**, **StandUP** and **ShowUP**, in partnership with Stand 4 Sisterhood, will become exclusive members of our **StandUP Society**.

For more info about our initiatives, please visit our website: www.stand4sisterhood.org

In Loving Memory of…..

Michael Borland
"Uncle Mike"
You were a light that shined so bright and could light up a room.
You are truly missed. We love you.
Audrey Borland, Marlon and Narae Borland, Malik Borland
Love you all.

Karlene Atkinson
She was the most authentic, nurturing, hilarious person I knew and she is missed everyday.
Sending love to her family and friends.
Andrew Atkinson, Andrew Atkinson Jr., and Alahna Atkinson

Stephanie White
You were in my life from birth. You were loved and such a great person.
You are a beautiful soul that is truly missed.
Rose White and Nicholas White

THE EVOLUTION EFFECT

The Evolution Effect is a compilation of 20 stories of individuals who have taken a risk and a leap of faith in themselves. Individuals who are building a legacy and have made drastic changes in their life. We are sharing their stories to help others to face their own traumas, challenges, and overcome adversities. With our collection of stories, we focused on depression, domestic violence, divorce, mental and physical health challenges, sexual assault, childhood traumas. The sole purpose was to work together to share their stories and create a powerful book to impact and inspire millions of lives.

For more information and to purchase a copy visit www.evolutioneffectbook.com

Chapters Include:

"Watering The Right Seeds: Keep Growing"
By Co-Author - Kele Carter
Kele Web Designs: Digital Marketing Agency
www.kelewebdesigns.com

"Love Changed Me"
By Co Author - Sheldine Gordon
instagram.com/gordonsheldine

"Breaking The Mold"
By Co-Author – Jeneea Moore
instagram.com/savedoversucess

"The Journey to Finding ME Again"
By Co-Author - Monica Reed
Her Creative Corner: The Entrepreneur Business Center
www.HERBUSINESSCENTER.COM

"The Evolution Of Pain"
By Co-Author - Lindsey Vertner
Lindsey Vertner Global
Www.LindseyVertner.com

OUR TRUTH IS NOT A LIE

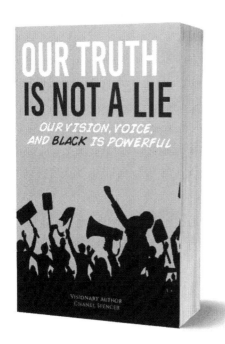

"Our Truth Is Not A Lie" is an audio and e-book with 18 compelling stories about the black and brown experience. There are often times our experiences are suppressed and unaddressed. When we share our truths it is either disregarded or minimized. Our Truth is Not A Lie and you will hear us loud and clear. Our voices, visions, and black are ALL powerful and beautiful. We deserve to more than matter. We have all worked extremely hard to change the narrative and build a legacy. Listen to our stories.

For more information and to purchase a copy visit www.ourtruthbook.com

Chapters Include:

"Non-Toxic Behavior"
By Co-Author – Lentheus Chaney
instagram.com/lentheuschaney

"Success Does Not Have A Color"
By Co-Author – Kettia Green
Hey SK Love
https://comesayheysk.info

"From Trauma To Power Purpose"
By Co-Author – Taniesha Ramsey-Lane
CEO Diva Enterprise LLC
www.CEO-DIVA.live

"Rewriting the Narrative"
By Co-Author – Lavar Thomas
Empower For Greatness
www.lavarthomas.com

ME
PUBLISHING
CHILDREN'S CORNER

THE LIFE OF HARPER

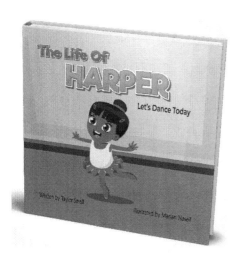

In this book, you will meet Harper. She absolutely loves dance. Join her as she has a full day of ballet and gymnastics with her friends. Come and have some fun with her!! You are invited.

Find out more at www.TJPlayword.com

THE ADVENTURES OF CJ

In this book, you will meet CJ. He has a super-secret. His parent's has super powers…shhhh. You can't tell anyone. Join CJ on his great adventure. As he learns how special and powerful, he truly is.

Find out more at www.TJPlayword.com

Made in the USA
Middletown, DE
31 March 2025

73478698R00125